THE JOURNEY OF
Healing Hearts

GLORIA J NELSON

WESTBOW
PRESS®
A DIVISION OF THOMAS NELSON
& ZONDERVAN

WestBow Press books may be ordered through booksellers or by contacting:

WestBow Press
A Division of Thomas Nelson & Zondervan
1663 Liberty Drive
Bloomington, IN 47403
www.westbowpress.com
844-714-3454

ISBN: 978-1-6642-3173-3 (sc)
ISBN: 978-1-6642-3174-0 (e)

Print information available on the last page.

WestBow Press rev. date: 05/05/2021

Gloria Nelson's devotional book is designed to help you, the reader, receive personal encouragement and spiritual empowerment as you navigate through everyday life. From the overflow of her relationship with God, the experiences of her personal journey and insights gleaned from time helping others Gloria helps you forge a path towards personal healing and ultimate freedom. The Bible says that there are "Many voices in the world and none of them without significance ". Gloria's voice, read in the pages this book, will help lead you to 'the voice' in whom we all find help and healing; the Lord Jesus Christ. Read and listen.

Lynton Turkington
Senior Pastor
Celebration Church
Raleigh North Carolina

The first step to healing is to know you are not alone!

Acknowledging that you are not alone can make the pain and hurt relatable to others, open you up to listen how others have dealt with this same thing and have survived.

There are others who have traveled this road of hurt and pain. Reach out to find a good support group.

Don't ignore the hurt and pain, face it head on with support of a group leader or counselor. Group therapy is amazing.

Acknowledging this is a process it is a series of actions or steps taken in order to achieve a particular end...healing!

There are no quick fixes, it is a journey of healing. All of the ugliness, hurt, muck and mire; have to be sifted through...but ahh on the other side is peace, healing and yes, joy.

Forgiveness not only the people who hurt you but forgive yourself; the gift of forgiveness releases you from being bound up. It truly is a gift.

Read, read and read more start with the word of God. Get self-help books specific to the pain you are dealing with. Knowledge is power but God's wisdom is like a starburst opening up your spirit to endless healing.

Immerse yourself in the Word. Listen to praise and worship music. Open the blinds in your home, let the sun shine in. Get out of the house, take a walk, exercise (even though you don't want to) and breathe and exhale.

Straighten your crown, stand tall as the child of God that you are. The King, our Creator calls you His.

The above is just a few of the first steps of your healing journey. Don't you want to be in with a group of women who have been hurt and just want to heal?

Are you ready to allow God to walk with you through this journey?

I've been done wrong. I am mad, angry, and I want revenge. I just want them to hurt as much as they have hurt me. I want to punch them, I...I... just want them to feel pain.

Let's think about that and take it apart 1 by 1. You've been done wrong by someone. God says revenge is mine. Take it in your own hands and you are prone to sin. Paul writes about anger; he says if you are angry be sure it is not sinful anger. Don't give the devil a foothold. Answer...take your anger to God, let Him be your Avenger.

I am mad, is it wrong to be mad? No, Paul is making a point that misdirected anger opens a door to the enemy to come into your life. Jesus showed us there is a place for righteous anger.

Gossip is a reputation destroyer. Gossip comes from the English word Go sip, when the politicians (when computers, newspapers and other modern technology wasn't around) they would send people into the pubs and tell them to go sip and find out what the people are saying. Gossip can destroy a reputation.

Have you ever been talked about at work and it wasn't true? This can make you extremely angry, mad and make you want to act out in an unrighteous way.

We are living in this world but we are not of this world. When unrighteous anger gets a hold of you STOP!

Take it to God and ask Him to go before you, make right your name, and to be your Advocate. Ask Him to reveal the unrighteous ones, ask Him to let the truth be revealed. Ask Him to expose the lie.

Then sit back, take your hands off it, forgive and watch your God move that mountain.

Ask God to help you to honor Him today.

Healing your broken heart. Where to start? First acknowledge the hurt and pain; give it a name so it can't mask or morph into something else.

If the pain is from years ago, more than likely it has turned into something else. Anger, sadness, depression, addiction...and now you are at the point either something has to change or God help me.

There is help out there. Help is not going to knock on your door while you seclude yourself away. You have to seek out that help. Hard to do when the pain is so overwhelming...but reach out you must. Talk to someone, open up to someone, call out to your Father to direct you to that one person who can help.

When we are emotionally depleted, we have nothing left to give. Our bank account is in a deficit. What do you do? You have to make deposits into your emotional account. Stop making withdrawals!

Lean on God, Christian friends and family. Start reconnecting, take baby steps, and... just begin again.

There is healing, there is forgiveness and there is a new morning each day for a fresh start. Stop allowing the enemy to steal from you. Hasn't he stolen enough!

Today, I pray for anyone not feeling like you are enough, unworthy of love, friendship or even kindness. He says you are!

I Am who I Am... what do you call Him? God, the Father, Creator or ABBA Daddy?

Is your relationship so close that you call Him Pappa?
In the movie, The Shack, God appears to the husband Mack, as Himself, Jesus and the Holy Spirit. But He also showed Himself as a woman when Mack needed nurturing and then showed Himself as a man when Mack needed a Father's strength.

The Great I Am is who you need Him to be in times of trouble or times of sheer delight. Call upon Him:

Almighty God (El Shaddai) the All Sufficient One
Alpha and Omega
Ancient of Days
Beautiful and Glorious
Bread of Life
Beloved Son
Christ Jesus, the Hope in us
Comforter
Defense of my life
Deliverer
Does not change
Everlasting Light
Faithful
Gift of God
God of Glory
God of Truth
He is for us
He who searches minds and hearts
Helper

This is just A-H and just a few names of God. Learn them, call them out through this journey of life.

Let Him be there for you. Call upon Him just by crying out... oh my Lord and Savior, I need my Helper today. Give me Peace, give me the Favor of man in my workplace. Heal my sickness and diseases. Expand my territory. I can do nothing without You. You are my Author and Finisher of my faith. Strengthen my heart, Holy Spirit come with me throughout my day. My Trust, my Refuge, my Rock, I put my trust in You. Thank you, my Redeemer, for all You do for me. May I be a vessel that you can use today. In Jesus name I pray, Amen.

Ever feel like Job? I pray you never do but, when the enemy comes in like a flood, the Lord shall lift up a standard against him.

Ever see flood waters? It just overtakes the entire area. Water finds the path of least resistance. Did you hear that?

Well, I am NOT going to be the path of least resistance. I am going to stand against this flood with my armor of God on, yielding my sword and speaking God's word over my situation. Not today Satan, not today!

My God is bigger than all of this, His word does not return void, He is already surrounding me, protecting me...do you hear that Satan! You have no authority in my life, my finances, my job, my health, my marriage...you are under my feet and I tell you now GET THEE BEHIND ME IN JESUS NAME! All the Glory to God.

Everything changes, nothing remains the same, except our God.

Does change make you anxious? Are you open to change? Without change, growth is impossible.

Are you comfortable where you are? Or are you hungry for what God has for you?

Throughout the Bible God tells us to go, move, do good...its always forward, life is meant to be fruitful and multiple. We are not meant to move backwards, we walk forward, life's cycle is always forward.

We are born as babies, we grow, learn and change in so many ways. If you are not comfortable with change, ask God to help you with that.

Face change with grace, position yourself to accept this wonderful journey of growth. We can't stay babies and drink milk all our lives. We have to grow and mature and begin eating food.

Face this day with the Bread of Life, start with the best Spirit-filled food, His word! He will set your path straight and open you up to change.

Accept what was and appreciate what will be. Get excited about your life. It is meant to live!

We only have now, this moment...what will you do with it? As for me and my house, we shall serve the Lord.

Fear is a liar; it will tell you that you don't measure up. You're too fat, too dumb, not good enough. If you give into it, your thoughts will run wild and you will start acting as if it were true.

So, what if you conquer that fear with what He says about you? Take every thought into captivity. You're getting ready for a job interview, you're nervous and the fear sets in... what if they don't like me. What if I don't say the right things and oh no; if there is a test I'm going to fail.

Change it all by saying, I can do all things through Christ Jesus. I am the apple of my Father's eye. He goes before me and makes my way with the interviewer. I will in Jesus's name ace this interview.

See how speaking positive totally takes away the negative! Where does your identity come from today?

Can it be that easy? Try it, yes the Power is in the spoken word... speak it out!

In all things and in all decisions: PUSH

P RAY
U UNTIL
S OMETHING
H APPENS

Some days the road to healing may seem too long to travel, you are weary and just have had it...you wake up in the same jail cell of pain and misery, but if you do a self-check; you realize you are further along. You have been moved from that one prison to another that has hope.

Just like that...the decision is yours, do I continue or just stop?

Psalm 118:24 says; "this is the day the Lord has made; we will rejoice and be glad in it."

It is a choice; we make daily choices that can greatly impact your world. Hope you should never lose sight of it. It is in the Hope that makes us keep fighting. The Hope of Love, the Hope of better days ahead, The Hope of this journey, is making me a better person and the Hope of the world is Christ Jesus.

So, when the road gets long, when you are weary and ready to quit...remember the Hope of Christ Jesus with-out stretch hands is there walking alongside you. Reach out!

You've heard this saying before right (below). Is it really that easy? Test it out, the next time you get offended, don't take it on and consciously choose to respond differently and see if you can do the 90%.

Each time the 10% happens, stop, breathe (deep ones) and choose to respond differently. These are simple cognizant behavior choices you make along the way to direct your focus on the positive rather than the negative.

Is this easy to do...NO! But you can do it if you train yourself to let go of the offense, pain, and bitterness.

Isn't it time? Haven't these emotions stolen enough from you?

Let it go, speak to the pain and tell it, to go in Jesus's name. Speak to the spirit of offense and tell it that it no longer has a hold on you by the blood of Jesus. Command bitterness to uproot itself out of you by the authority you have in Jesus!

Matthew 16:19 "I will give you the keys of the kingdom of heaven; whatever you bind on earth will be bound in heaven, and whatever you lose on earth will be loosed in heaven."

Expectations exactly what is it? Can it be good or bad?

Webster Dictionary describes it as strong belief that something will happen or be the case in the future. "reality had not lived up to expectations" A belief that someone will or should achieve something.

If we set our standard of expectations too high, we can be disappointed if they are not met. The unmet expectations can leave you feeling frustrated, angry or void, because you were... well expecting something different.

In the Bible expectations differ from hope, "My soul, wait thou only on God, for my expectation is from him." Psalms 62:5. Our expectations in God to deliver should be met with high expectations because He is Sovereign and His Word never returns void.

However, when we expect high standards from humans, we should be ready for disappointment because we are...well human, flawed, sinful nature and some just cannot rise to your standard.

If you are expecting you from others, you will be disappointed, because no one else is you.

Does that mean you lower your expectations or standards? No, you expect the standard in which that individual can deliver. Listen, we all can't be A students. Some students work really hard for that C grade.

The Bible says:

In the Old Testament "expectation" always means that which is expected, as Proverbs 10:28, "The expectation of the wicked shall perish."

So, expect less from man and more from God. Pray with expectation that He answers prayers. Our Hope, our Provider, our Protector, our Creator, the One and Only God.

When you deflect, you throw someone or something off course, often by using a distraction. Another way to deflect something — such as criticism — is to blame someone else.

Denial is a coping mechanism that gives you time to adjust to distressing situations — but staying in denial can interfere with treatment or your ability to tackle challenges. If you're in denial, you're trying to protect yourself by refusing to accept the truth about something or someone that's happening in your life.

Denial is an attempt to cope, rationalize, or excuse behaviors in one way or another. It refers to failing to acknowledge an unacceptable emotion or truth. Denial can sometimes seem irrational, but it is used as a defense mechanism against situations or circumstances that are painful and overwhelming.

When we deflect and stay in denial (truth about ourselves or situation) we are stuck and cannot grow. Some stay here for years, the only way to move past this is to take off the veil and face the truth.

As difficult as it may be to see ourselves, only the truth shall set you free. It is not always someone's else's fault. We have to take the mirror of truth and look at ourselves.

Do I do that? Do I say that? Do I only speak to get my point across? Do I speak just to respond? Do I deflect? Is it easier to blame someone for your troubles?

The inward journey is about you, not anyone else. Finding out your why, your how and your emotional maturity.

A difficult journey for sure, to say could it be me, but a journey we all must take if we want to heal, do and be something different in our life. Get unstuck...

Sometimes, I wake up with a message to write. Other times, I sit quietly and ask the Lord to give me something. I wake up at 5, take my cup of coffee, have Alexa, play some soft praise songs and close my eyes and ask him to give it to me from my heart. Some mornings are easy, I wake with writings on my heart and poof I write it so quickly.

This morning was a difficult one, so Lord Jesus speak to my heart to write what you would love your children to hear. Anytime the Lord speaks I am humbled and honored to be used of Him to bring you His words, not mine.

He wants you to rise up in the morning and say good morning my Lord. He wants the 1st of your morning to fellowship with you. He desires relationship with you.

Just talk to him. Oh Lord you know I have that pesky neighbor, or worker, or my husband. Keep my eyes above the waves today, that all I can see is your love for me and keep me from speaking anything derogatory. Give me peace and love in my heart for that person _____ (name them). Lord lead me today with your Holy Spirit that I may be led by you and not my flesh

Every fiery dart that aimed at me today, you take it and turn it back on the one that called it my Father God.

Surround me and my family today, with your warrior angels in our comings and in our goings. I lift up my husband, today expand his territory Lord Jesus. You will never fail us, stronger are you Lord, surround my daughters, son in law, and our grandbabies, reconcile them back to you Lord

You are for us, you will not forsake us, you are fighting for us oh God. Thank you for this time to start my day with you father God.

I pray for every person reading this that your holy hand touches them and they are made whole. You know my needs lord they are great, but you are greater my Lord. I trust You Jesus!

Thank you, Lord, for hearing my prayer this morning for my family, this great nation we are in your hands, in Jesus's name. My unstoppable God go forth and heal this land and the broken hearted. We bind and rebuke the spirit of rebellion in this nation in Jesus's name. Soften the hearts of the people Abba Father. We need You; we need You now Father. Give us the strength to keep fighting and stay in your word daily. Praise your Holy name amen!

We sometimes have to go through the fire to become refined. Like gold; the impurities rise to the top. Diamonds are pressed, olives are pressed and we need to learn a lesson each and everyday.

Throughout the Bible there are struggles, sickness and even death...but with God, He shows us His promises and victories. The Bible isn't just for those days 2000-4000 years ago. It lives and breathes life into us today.

Those who read it find salvation, healing and a new way of living with joy, peace and understanding.

God says test me in these things. How dare we test the Creator of all? He wants us to so that He can reveal Himself to you. He surrounds us, He lives on the inside, He's got us covered.

Prayers release our faith and God reacts to our faith. Testimony after witnesses today of His love, grace and mercy for His children cannot be ignored. Real interactions with God Almighty through the blood of Jesus so that we can come before Him and lay our petitions at the Cross and let Him take the wheel. Relationship with Him...nothing better!

He takes the broken pieces and puts us back together, better than before. I may be cracked, but He has filled my broken pieces with His gold.

Get EXCITED today! It's a new morning to put on the full armor of God and get out there with a victorious attitude.

Your God goes before you to make your way straight. He walks with you. He fights for you. He is ready, willing and VERY ABLE, when you are weak, He is strong.

Make today count by going to Him 1st and giving Him this day. Watch the difference, take it out of your hands and put it in His.

Whew, just think you don't have to do it. Not today Satan...my God has got this!

I don't know how to move past this hurt and pain. I go to bed with it and wake up daily with it. How do I make it stop?

Healing! It's a process, a series of steps that propels you to the state of being healed. No quick fixes here, like surgery you are cut, bleed and then sewn or stapled back up. Then comes the healing process which is painful and just takes time. The wound oozes with puss and blood. The body part needs physical therapy to get moving again. The area turns black and blue, then scars. Sounds delightful right?

But this is the same journey that has to be taken with your emotional pain and scars. Some of you have been carrying it around for years. So, it may take years to heal. The scared tissue is so thick around it, it may need surgery again to cut it out. If you don't get to the root, you will be hacking at the leaves and never get to the reason why.

This is the journey of Healing Hearts...going deep to the root of your hurt, doing some surgery on it, dealing with it...some physical therapy and then learning the tools to get past it.

Through Christ who strengthens you, you can do all things. This will take believing and faith that God's got this.

On the other side of this is healing and He gives beauty for ashes! The Bible tells us to be laborers together with God 1 Co 3-9. You can't do this alone, in Healing Hearts and with God's word, we journey together learning how to release the hurt and pain and get this behind us.

Thank you Jesus that you are the driver in this journey. Thank You for what you did for us on the cross. Because of You we are healed in Jesus's name.

Now, let's apply it to our lives. It takes action on your part. You have to do the work to get better!

In a world where everyone wears a mask, isn't it awesome we get to see people's souls in church. They come hurt and broken to hear God's word. They come hungry for Him.

Probably why God loves us so much because He doesn't see our outer mask, but our hearts. And because He created us. We are His children.

Wouldn't it be wonderful if we all saw each other's heart condition? We could tell if the persons intentions are honorable or if it is deceitful.

Alas, only our Lord can see our heart condition. Getting to know yourself, you can ask yourself beforehand, am I angry, am I disappointed, or are am I hurting that I want others to hurt that you want others to hurt as bad as you?

Things said in jest are meaningful, if you listen you can hear. Ephesians 4:25 "let each of you speak truth.

I would much rather have a friend who speaks truth to me then a yes friend. There is where you grow and learn. It is where we become better. Is it painful to learn things about ourselves, yes! Don't get stuck, remove the mask, and check your heart condition today.

God's mercies are new every morning. We get a new page to write on. What will yours say today?

How do you pray? Is it a 5-minute conversation with God or do you war in your prayer closet?

To your Heavenly Father, He is elated to hear from you. Like your aging parents waiting by the phone to get the call from their children...He waits to hear from you.

So, whether you are going through a spiritual battle or just want to say good morning Father...He wants your prayers. Pray without ceasing.

The Great I Am is waiting to be what you need of Him at this time. Peace, Hope, Love, Grace, Mercy, Favor...what do you have need of today?

Go ahead start your day off right by calling out to ABBA Daddy, tell Him what you need.

It's grey outside and that's the way I feel inside. Blah... just about sums it up. I don't feel like doing anything. Staying inside just wallowing in this grey space.

Have you ever felt this way? This is one step away from the darkness over shadowing you. A place we all get to, the answer is to acknowledge it and get out quickly.

How, how do you get out? Remind yourself there is ALWAYS hope.

Get dressed, get up, get out of the house. Put headphones on, play praise music and go for a walk, a drive...reach out to a person of God. You are not alone! You have a Savoir who is there to walk alongside you. Lift your hands and thank Him for all the positive things you have. They are there...you have to look for them. Ask Him to show you all the good in your life.

Change your lenses in which you are seeing out of. Clean them off and see that He is a God of Hope, Change is possible.

He will take your mess, your pain and turn it into something beautiful. Give Him a chance...this is your Hope! Jesus Christ.

Did you know that cheating is not just a sexual affair? Whenever a spouse goes to another, and takes away from the spouse, it is straying away from the marriage.

We tend to think of a sexual affair is cheating. But what if sex is not involved? Is there such a thing as emotional cheating? The answer is yes; when you have conversations with another (of the opposite sex), confiding in them, you take away, what is meant for your spouse; the intimacy of communication, exchanging thoughts, communicating hurts and happiness should be with your spouse first.

Let's go back to when you both first met, what was it that attracted you? Visually appealing, great conversation, dating, going out doing things together and intimacy (doesn't mean sexual)? See you had that at the beginning, lots of great communication. What happened? What is it yelling instead of listening to understand?

If you find yourselves in a dry spell in your marriage, or name calling...STOP! Go back to the beginning, remind each other, what made you fall in love with your spouse. Turn your heart back towards your partner.

There is nothing better than when a man and woman places God 1st, spouse 2nd, children 3rd, and then work. When this is out of balance, our marriage is out of balance. Put things back into perspective and get that marriage you both wanted when you said I do!

It is possible if you both want it and work hard on the partnership. All things are possible through Christ Jesus.

It is so easy to get ourselves worked up and let our emotions get the best of us. The bible shows us the answer. Isaiah 26:3 You will keep him in perfect peace, who mind is stayed on You.

It is easier for us to get caught up in our thoughts when something happens. Our minds wander, what if. We worry, get stressed and we become miserable.

It is harder to do it according to the bible (but really so simple) which is get out of our natural self, our flesh and get in the spirit.

We need to see, touch and feel to believe it's real. But our eyes can deceive us, our thoughts conjure up things that aren't even happening yet and we're miserable with grief and worry.

Keep your peace and allow God in your situation and take yourself out of the equation. Watch Him move that mountain for you. It is always amazing to watch Him move on your behalf.

Testimony after testimony all the Glory to God for He is so good! Let go today, give it to Him. His yoke is easy, our burdens are too heavy for us.

Thank you Lord Jesus for Your Comforter.

Jealousy is an emotion that is not healthy for you or the other person. It makes you suspicious envious, covetous, or desirous; feeling or showing suspicion of someone's unfaithfulness in a relationship. James 3:16 says disorder happens when there is jealousy. Proverbs 14:30 a tranquil heart gives life to the flesh, but envy makes the bones dry.

Synonyms: suspicious, distrustful, mistrustful, doubting, insecure, or anxious. When feeling this way about someone sets you in an emotional tailspin.

It is not good for you or anyone else in your life. Examine your WHY in this, find out and get this out of you as soon as possible, it will not serve you well.

God's word tells us not to covet others wives, husbands or even stuff. When you see someone succeed; what is your reaction? Is it one of genuine congratulatory pleasure, or I wish it was me?

Do you realize how much work went into that leadership role? How hard that person studied to get to that role? How much time and effort they had to sacrifice, or how many years it took them to get there?

Today, with stars in our eyes and instant gratification all we want it now! But when we see someone being elevated, taken from Glory to Glory, are we truly happy for them, or do you say that should have been me?

Listen, if God can't trust you in the small stuff, He's not going to give you the big stuff. Get rid of that jealousy fast! It serves no one any good, replace it with an attitude of gratitude, true and pure excitement for the other person. For it wasn't in an instant that they were elevated, it was years of reproof, work, tears and pain.

Clap with absolute joy for them that you can now learn from them. And if you want it, you too can be elevated. God is not a respecter of any one person but He does want you to show Him you can be trusted with such an important job.

He cares about who is feeding His people. He cares who is leading His people. He has elevated them to help you! Listen and learn from them. Then apply it to your life and grow.

We each have gifts and talents that the body of Christ needs. 1 person can't do it alone. The body of Christ needs many hands. Are you ready to grow, go through the journey of healing and being mentored?

What are your gifts and talents that you can use to help advance the body of Jesus Christ?

He doesn't want you drinking milk all the time. He wants to see you grow and start eating meat. He's waiting to advance you. Are you ready to grow?

Jeremiah 32:27...do you believe? If you do, hold onto this verse and when you pray just believe it is done.

He says if you have the faith of a mustard seed, say to the mountain...move and it will.

What is your mountain today? Job, finances, health, reconciliation... is there anything too difficult for Him?

The answer is NO! When you pray believe that He is capable and willing to answer your prayer. Oh, but wait, it's His timing, it is always perfect.

Listen, sometimes you may pray for years, other times your prayer is answered quickly. I prayed for 12 years for my spouse. You don't know what God is doing on both sides getting you both ready for one another.

Same with a job, you don't know what He is doing opening the right job in the natural for you.

So, never cease praying, never lose faith, declare and decree that prayer with expectation, it is yours in Jesus's name!

Let patience have its perfect work...James 1:3

Do you? We are so impatient today with everything and everyone. We want it now! We think people should act like us, know exactly what it is that we want, what we know, and we get frustrated when they take too long.

I had someone call me and said I emailed you 10 minutes ago and you haven't answered me!

Our instant society, our wanting answers now, just Google it, has made us a society of impatient people, a push of the button and we have dinner ready. Some people don't even cook, or sit and have dinner at the table with family anymore.

Even in driving they think they own the road rather than sharing it with others at that time and space. Where they are going is more important than where any other driver is going. Watch out! I am driving here! I am more important and where I am going is more important than the other drivers sharing the road at that time with you.... hmmm patience.

Most of us desire change, desire improvement but we don't want to pay the price of patience.

To change requires growth, have you seen an infant come out and be a toddler? No, he/she has to grow and learn. You can't fast forward past the growing season. There is no button for this!

Dr. John Maxwell said "don't change enough to get away from your problem, change enough to solve them. Don't change your circumstances to improve your life, change yourself to improve your life".

The definition of insanity is doing the same thing over and over again excepting a different result. Do you?

Change, growth, resolution, going through it, making a difference, do something different...change your mindset! Be patient with yourself and others. This is where we start patience.

We can't circumvent the process, we can't escape life's problems, when we try, we cheat ourselves of learning, changing and growth. We end up with a bigger problem or pain...denial and avoidance.

Face it head-on, be open to change and be patient, let it have its perfect work in Christ Jesus.

Let's talk about color. The seven colors of the rainbow are red, orange, yellow, green, blue, indigo, and violet. A rainbow is God's promise to us. When you see one don't you marvel at its beauty? Even though we only see 1/2 of the rainbow, it truly is a complete circle. A rainbow has to be at the right angle and positioned on the opposite side of the sun in order for us to see it.

God's beautiful artistic paint brush uses different colors for flowers, grass (yes, even grass has different color greens) birds, and animals; the list goes on and on. So, why then, when we see the majestic colors are we in awe of their beauty? The male duck is colorful, while the female is demure. Does that make her any less beautiful?

God does not see the color of our skin. He made us brown, black, white, yellow or olive skin tone...there are so many different tones of our skin. We are all beautiful in His sight; He made us! Does a mother and father after giving birth to their child say ugh to the sight of their newborn? No! They are the most beautiful and awesome thing they have ever seen.

God sees us all as His creation, His children...when He looks at us, He doesn't see our skin but our hearts; the condition of our heart. Is your bitter? Is your broken or hurt? Is yours angry or filled with rage? Why then, when we are with a group that is different than us, are we skeptical? Birds of a feather flock together?

Maybe you need to expand your group, get out of your comfort zone and see others as beautiful as God sees them. Again, the female duck is still a duck; so are we, all a part of the human race. Take our skin off and we all look the same underneath.

But God being the artist made us all different beautiful colors. If we were all the same color; if the earth didn't have color, we'd live in a grey world. How boring and dreadful.

Celebrate the colors of the world, thank God, He made us all beautiful in His sight.

Jeremiah 1:5 before I formed you in your mother womb, I knew you...

Gratitude...this one word that can encourage a marriage to continue, or can show someone you care. Even God wants to hear thank you after answering your prayer.

In relationships it is easy to take the other for granted. You treat strangers better than you do your own family.

Being thankful changes a heart condition. Turns negative into positive.

We need to have an attitude of gratitude each day. Even when the tides turn or when the storm passes, the sun returns and there is a beauty afterwards.

God has given you a new morning, this morning! What will you do with this new day? Carry your yesterday worries and troubles into this new day? Or will you turn the page and start a new one with positive words of encouragement? This is not just for others, but encouragement for you too.

Today, I choose to be positive, encouraging and to have an attitude of gratitude, how about you?

Lord Jesus, thank you for another day to be a blessing. Alert me through the Holy Spirit when you put someone in my path that I need to encourage. Thank you for all you do for me even when I am unaware. My Jesus, my Savior, today I have gratitude.

Are you controlling or do you know someone who is dominating?

Exercising supremacy over someone is not our right or place. People are not to be owned but to be loved, taught and allowed to live. Jesus did not control, but showed us how to pray, live, and love one another by being a servant from the heart.

A great leader is when the people prosper. A controlling leader; the people are enslaved. Jesus set people free! A true leader, leads from the heart, pours into people, does NOT take away.

Are you controlling in your relationships? Listen, the only thing we can control is ourselves, what comes out of our mouths, our reaction or better yet...no reaction or response.

Stop expecting YOU from others. They are not you! We love differently, we all are a product of where and how we grew up. We are all unique. Begin appreciating the gifts in one another.

Pour into your partner, be of service from your heart...be the helpmate God created you to be. Did you know the Holy Spirit is our Helpmate? That is the type of heart we should have in helping others...from the Heart, pouring into others, not taking away.

Once you get this into your soul God will rest upon you and you will be elevated to new heights in your relationships.

If you are all about performance you are task oriented...learn to love and lead from your heart and others will follow.

True, kingdom-style leadership means pouring yourself into someone else's life for their benefit. Leadership isn't about the title next to your name; it's about your authority and anointing in the spiritual realm to empower those around you. That is in our marriage, friendships, and all relationships empowering people. Control takes away and creates diversity. Empowering adds to and creates a thankfulness.

Today, pray that God removes the anger and control that has been controlling you and replaced it with a giving and loving heart.

Does worrying change anything? Does being anxious about anything help? Does complaining about anything changes things?

The answer to all of the above is No! While you are complaining about your spouse, there are those who just lost theirs. While you are anxious about your test, there are those who can't afford to go to school, and while you worry about your job, there are those who just lost theirs.

We live in a world of hurting people. The person who looks like they have it all together could be holding on by a thread, so broken inside that one more thing could push them over the edge.

A complaining person spreads negativity to all those who will hear, it is contagious. Hurt people, hurt people, but an encourager spreads positivity and changes the thought pattern in others.

Being polite and positive changes perspective, change the lens in which you see your circumstances and you will change your circumstance.

There are many books about this that all stem from the Biblical principle...be anxious for nothing! We are already victorious, Jesus Christ has gone before us and made a way for you.

So, next time you want to complain about your parents, praise God you have them still. Next time your child bothers you, praise God you have them...we can always change our perspective which will change your outcome.

Today...see how many people you can help with being an encourager with positive words. It will make you happy and change you forever.

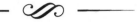

Each day of your life has 1,440 minutes. God deserves a few of them; and you deserve the experience of spending a few quiet minutes every morning with Him.

So, if you haven't already established the habit of spending time with God every day of the week, it is time for you to start.

It's a habit that will change your day and revolutionize your life when you give the Lord your undivided attention everything changes including you.

Not a bad few minute of your time. Go ahead put Him 1st and watch your life change.

Lord, I give you this day. Help me to be a better stewart of my time and finances. Make me better at time management. I commit not only my 1st fruits but my 1st minutes of my day to you.

Ever been so tired you can't even pray? Walking in a place of dryness, a desert where you don't know even how to pray?

We all have been there, you know...where you wonder where is God. We call that desert times.

There were times all I could do is cry out Jesus, Jesus, Jesus, my God, my God, help me! Yep, that's it, that was all I had.

These are the times we have to encourage ourselves in the Lord. Like King David did in the caves. Read Psalms where he would cry out. Oh Lord why have you forsaken me! BUT then you read where he shouts out to the Lord with praise.

We all go into the dry dark places. We all need to get ourselves out of there too. Remember building alters (journaling) remembering what God has done for you in the past is a good place to start.

God doesn't pull away from us, we pull away from Him. We made a choice, a decision that somewhere it brought us to that desert.

Now get back on track and begin to praise Him and enter into the throne room with Thanksgiving, Worship and Praise. He is nearer than you know. He never leaves us, He sustains us. He is waiting for you to draw near to Him.

Like a Father waiting at home to talk with you, waiting to hug you. He's waiting to Love on you...oh my, run don't walk into His arms. Praise you Father, thank you for your Love, Mercy and Grace! Amen

Even when we don't know it or realize it God has our back. Remember His timing is not ours...in a twinkling of an eye...is a thousand years for our Lord.

When we pray remember that His timing is perfect, may help you not to get frustrated. We live in the natural realm our God is Spirit. Our days turn into weeks, month and yes sometimes years...God is working on your prayer request.

Why can't God do it right then and there? He could, but depending on your prayer (for a spouse or a job, etc.) He has to go into the future to get it/them ready for you. He is history and He is the future. Perhaps the right spouse for you needs work right now but in 1 year, or so will be ready for you. Then He will present your Adam or Eve.

No matter what your prayer is today...remember God's got this. Pray in the hallway until that door opens. Pray His Will be done in all things. If it is not of God, I don't want it. He is a Good Father; He's got your back!

Do you remember all the things that God has done for you since your walk with Him? Probably not, in the old testament they would build small alters of stones along their path (walk or journey). They said let us build an alter and remember what God has done for us.

We too need to remind ourselves of the wonderful things He has done along our journey. Of course, today we don't have to put stones together, but we should journal or use your smartphone in notes and remind yourself of what He has done for you. Read it often, what He has done for you? Thank Him, He's a good Father!

We are all moving about so quickly today, that we forget yesterday or even last week. Begin to journal, you will shift your attitude to gratitude once you realize how good our Father is.

Begin to thank Him for answered prayer, or for that matter, even unanswered prayer. Seeing those things that are not, as if they are! Expectation that He gives to His children what we need.

His unanswered prayer can be a blessing too, because He sees what it could do to us. What lesson is He teaching you? If you are facing a mountain (struggle) ask Him, Lord what are you trying to teach me here?

Father, today I ask for forgiveness and I come humbly before You with gratitude for Your Mercy, Grace and Love of Your children. I praise You for all things in my life. Even the mountain that You have assigned to me to move through faith I speak to it now in Jesus's name be thou removed. All the Glory to You my Heavenly Father. Amen

Do you really know who you are? We often relate ourselves to what we do, I'm a doctor, a schoolteacher, I'm a nurse, a mother... is that who you are?

Think about that for a minute, who are you really? The above is your profession, or responsibility. It's what you do for a living. It is not who you are. So again, I ask who are you?

The enemy knows who you are, he knows your triggers, what buttons to push, your weaknesses, so you better get to know yourself!

This is about knowing who you are at your core. Understanding and recognizing your deeper self.

As kids we emulate our parents, then we get into our teenage years and fall to peer pressure. When do we get to know ourselves? 20's, 30's, 40's is it our 50's? Do we ever get to really know our core self?

We usually figure out some of who we are through much trials and pain. It's how we learn and grow. We figure out our strengths and weaknesses. But when it comes to the truth about our negative qualities, we don't want to see ourselves, but we must in order to overcome.

Taking personal inventory of our strengths and weaknesses is a step towards improving ourselves. It's painful to admit...am I really that way? Do I really do that? Am I controlling? Do I dominate?

The first step towards healing is admitting, coming out of denial, it is the only way to begin to heal and become a better person. Forgive and let go of anger, accept your role in the situation, and stop blaming others. Take personal inventory.

We take back our life when we understand our responsibility in our actions. We can only control ourselves, your words that come out of your mouth and how you react to a situation. That's it!

We try to numb our pain; it only masks the situation for a while. Sooner or later, we have to face it head on. Don't let it take root in your spirit. Deal with it when it happens. When the enemy comes in like a flood, the Lord shall lift up a standard against him. Call it out in Jesus's name.

Pray: Lord I have wasted enough of my life-giving others too much say so in my life. Help me to see who I am. Take the Holy ghost flashlight into the chambers of my heart and reveal to me the things I must forgive, the people I must forgive, help me oh Lord, to become a better person, to really know myself so I can finish this journey strong and be who you called me to be. Be with me through this journey of healing. When I am scared to face a reality, let me know to cross that line will bring about truth and healing. When I struggle, show me that over that mountain is a new me in Jesus's name. You Father God are with me through the fire and I will come out unburned. Praise you Father who sustains me. I am ready Lord to heal, see me, the real me and begin applying your Word to my life! Amen.

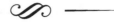

Do you appreciate your spouse? Do you show them in special ways? Or do you expect and take for granted what they do for you?

The 1st part of my marriage was not good. Communication was non-existent, words of appreciation weren't spoken, quality of time wasn't shared and words of anger were shouted making everything worse. The marriage needless to say fell apart after 12 years and I left.

Control issues, anger issues and deep-rooted problems stemming from childhood were never resolved and reared its ugly head in those 12 years. Broken, hurt, betrayed and numb from it all, leaving was my choice, with lots of prayer.

God knew change would only take place in him if he saw all those things that I did which he took for granted. Cooking, cleaning, ironing, his laundry folded for him, and dinners ready when he got home. In our business the 70 hours that I worked trying to hold it all together just became too much for me, it was making me sick, depressed and miserable.

It's not that we didn't try counseling, many, many different counselors...but denial is a veil that keeps you blinded. Until you are ready to look inside yourself and you are sick of being sick, until the pain of staying the same is too much, no one can make a difference. It really does take two. And it is free will, if you are not willing to go deep and make the changes, you will remain the same.

We need to aspire to be better, to do better in all aspects of our life and in our marriage. It took 3.5 years of separation and today our marriage is strong, communication is plenty and we both encourage each other to be the best we can for each other.

But wait there's more...No, go back home and tell them what the Lord has done for you. Luke 8:39

None of this could have been achieved without our Lord! Our story is truly a miracle that we are back together again. In June we celebrated 20 years of marriage.

The morale of this story is that if you both want the marriage, you both pray and seek guidance, that a good solid marriage is attainable. It is work, daily work but the fruit of your work is delicious. A rock-solid happy marriage!

I am blessed to finish this life with this wonderful man of God who seeks to serve Him, but me as well. Makes me feel loved, special and like a queen, his queen.

Thank you Jesus for never leaving or forsaking us, thank You for putting the right people in our paths to sustain us and grow us during those 3.5 years of separation. Thank you for my husband today. You are a good, good Father!

Did you know cheating is not just sexual? Whenever a spouse goes to another and takes away from the spouse, it is straying away from the marriage.

We tend to think of an affair is cheating. But what if sex is not involved? Is there such a thing as emotional cheating? The answer is yes. When you have conversations with another (of the opposite sex), confiding in them, you take away what is meant for your spouse. That intimacy of communication, exchanging thoughts, hurts and happiness should be with spouse 1st.

Let's go back to when you both first met, what was it that attracted you? Visually appealing, great conversation, dating, going out doing things together and intimacy (doesn't mean sexual)? See you had that at the beginning.

If you find yourselves in a dry spell in your marriage, go back to the beginning, remind each other of what made you love your spouse. Turn your heart back towards your spouse.

There is nothing better than when a man and woman places God 1st, spouse 2nd, children, and then work. When this is out of balance our marriage is out of balance. Put things back into perspective and get that marriage you both wanted when you said I do!

Choose for yourself THIS day whom you will serve...as for me and MY house, we shall serve the Lord. Joshua 24:15

It is your choice, the world's way or God's way. It is yours alone to make.

How do you react to failure, that annoying customer, traffic, rude and rushing people?

How do you react to success, those you see losing weight or see getting promoted or getting honored?

It is our choice how we respond or react to yes, every situation. We have the power if you will, to change the outcome of every problem.

Think of a situation that wasn't your shining moment. What could you have done differently if you paused, breathed and responded in another way? Learn to do better, to control your emotions and take control over your thoughts. We can develop better listening skills, spiritual growth and emotional Intelligence.

Like all things it takes work, intention, and application to your journey of becoming a better you.

Don't be like the world rushing through life. Stop, think, pray and most of all enjoy the journey. God may have assigned this mountain to you...have the faith to move it, through Jesus Christ and learn the lesson that it is teaching you.

Can 1 word truly have the power to change things? Our words are containers of power that can tear down or build up. Yes, our words are powerful.

That small muscle in your mouth that has no bones is powerful enough to give life or death.

We never know what someone is going through.

A child needs to hear more positive reinforcement than all the things they do wrong. A spouse needs to hear the things you are proud of, what they did right, rather than all the negative. What about the singles in the world that may have no one to lean on.

Your words are powerful enough to give life or death to someone? Which will you choose this day?

Watch someone's face and demeanor change when you give a compliment. When the waitress/waiter comes to your table say hello, be kind. Let the mother in the store with the crying baby know she's doing a good job, she's already struggling. Your encouragement is what she needs rather than the evil look of being annoyed.

If you call your child even in jest, oh he's a monster, he'll grow up being a monster. Instead call him blessed, kind and loving.

Even your internal words you speak over yourself have the power to tear you down or give you strength. Ever hear a coach before a game? He doesn't call his team slackers; no, he builds them up before the game. He calls the powerful, winners!

Each morning before the game of life, start your morning in the Word of Life and speak out loud what your Heavenly Father calls you. Let the Coach of Encouragement gets you psyched up to get out and live this day.

You are the apple of ABBA Father's eye, His beloved, you are His royal priesthood, you are so loved by our King.

The only way to start your day, get dressed immerse yourself in God's word and watch your day be different today.

Be kind out there today. We are a world filled with hurt and angry people. Smile say something positive! Be an encourager.

Colossians 3:2 set your mind and keep focused habitually on the things above...

Don't stay focused on your circumstances. If you do, you stay stuck...there is no growth.

1 Cor 2:16 says we have the mind of Christ...this means no matter what our circumstances are, we have God's Wisdom, discernment and His Power with us and around us at all times to access it. Fight in the spirit.

Philippians 2:5 have the same attitude in yourselves which in Christ Jesus...look to Him as your example. In selfless humility, a person with a humble mind is a peaceful person.

The word says be anxious for nothing. So, what are you anxious today about?

Fear is a liar, take your problems vertical and let His Peace over take you. He has already won the battle!

Consider the book of Job; when we have 1 thing happen in life, we lose it. Can you imagine losing your lifetime of work and family in a matter of minutes? But Job never lost his faith.

Yesterday, I posted when the enemy comes in like a flood, this is not 1 event, it is a barrage of things happening over a period of time. What will your reaction be? We are human and will have to go through our emotions/feelings of the situation. But the key is to feel it quickly and then give it to God.

Job writes, 6:3-4; my words have been spoken fast and without thought. How many of us react like that? Then he writes, for the arrows of the All-powerful are in me. You have that Power.

What is the answer when we go through such troubled waters? Your life Savior walks on water! Go to the word, yes, feel it but don't get stuck. Quickly give it to Him, put on your armor and stand against the wiles of the enemy.

Speak His words out loud, not in your head. The power is in the spoken word. Job 5:20-21, He will keep you from death in times of no food, and from the power of the sword in times of war. You will be hidden from the punishment of the tongue.

Be not afraid, put your trust in Him and be at peace. He is working on your behalf. Today praise God for what you don't see.

God created the heaven and earth in 7 days, but on the 7th day He rested.

Being away for the 1st time in 2 years on a real vacation makes me see why God tells us to REST.

The past 2 years with Leadership at work, moving our office, moving into a new home, leadership at Celebration Church...I haven't had time to just rest.

This morning just waking up with no time restraints on where we go, what to do, just planning fun time together, makes me see you cannot pour from an empty vessel.

So, today plan a day this week just to rest. He calls us to do just that!

Have you ever been the target of gossip? Gossip can ruin a person's reputation by 1/2 truths mixed with lies.

The mouth spreading it is believed as if it were true. Why because they said it and spoke the words? Or because people want to believe the worst of people?

The one being slandered can be totally innocent and the mouth feeding the frenzy totally guilty. But who is being hurt from the lies?

King David had to hide away in the caves because Saul sought to kill him.

Our thoughts, words and our heart condition has to be checked daily. Once lies are spoken it is difficult for others to see the truth. Words are powerful containers. Why do most people want to believe the bad stuff? Psalms 1 says...or laugh at the truth. Gossip.

But we have to be like the tree planted by the water that gives fruit at the right time (God's timing).

Psalms 1:4 - 6 sinful men are not like this. They are like straw blown away by the wind. So, the sinful will not stand. They will be told they are guilty and have to suffer for it. Sinners will not stand with those who are right with God. For the Lord knows the ways of those right with Him.

The pain and turmoil of digging your way out of slander and gossip is hurtful and exhausting, but we serve a God who is ready to go to battle to vindicate you.

Don't fight it in the natural and make things worse. Fight it in the spirit and send a myriad of Angel's out on your behalf and watch the tide turn.

May every word spoken be revealed as a lie, may God turn every fiery dart aimed at you around to penetrate the ugly words spoken from the mouths that uttered them.

My God, my God you are my Advocate, my Counselor, my Banner. Take a stand against the enemy that is coming in like a flood. Vindicate me my Lord Jesus. All the praise and glory Jesus my Savior.

I was asked in my cGroup, are there hindrances to answered prayer? Yes, prayerlessness is one. You have not because you ask not Jas 4:3. Sounds simple right, God is waiting for your prayer.

Let us approach the throne of grace with confidence...Hebrews 4:16. Lack of confidence is a hindrance to answered prayer. I know God can do it, but I find it hard to believe He will do it for me. No, He can and will do it! Pray with expectation that you ask, God hears and His grace He gives to us.

If I have iniquity in my heart, the Lord will not hear me. Psalm 66:18. Sin is a hindrance. Pray asking Him to forgive you, then thank Him for forgiveness. Check yourself, the little things grow into habits.

If we ask anything according to His will, he hears us... 1 John 5:14. Praying outside of God's will is a hindrance. The best way to pray is according to His will. If it is not His will, I don't want it. Your will, oh Lord!

You do not receive because you ask with wrong motives...James 4:3. A motive is the "why" behind the asking.

A pure heart is what God is looking for. He sees our heart condition. We need to examine our heart daily.

Be sure when praying you are asking without hindrances. A hurt heart will never let the mind rest. If you have a hurting heart, seek out the root cause. Ask yourself the hard questions.

Praying God's will for our lives is always the answer we need.

Is the safest place to be is on the battlefield, when you are warring spiritually? King David didn't get into trouble with Bathsheba until he left the battlefield.

Keep fighting, endure (it's your staying power) ...after you've done all you can do... stand. But stand in faith, believing that God is with you.

Faith, believe, and trust even without the details of how. Now that's faith.

Keep moving forward trusting that our God will never leave you.

Persistence over comes resistance!

In general men are different than women. God made us that way. It would seem these differences not only attract us but is largely our downfall in misunderstandings and miscommunication in our relationship with them.

When women speak, especially to other women, we talk in stories, details and in depth from our feelings.

When men speak, they talk in headlines. Women will usually see the glazed over look after going on, from their spouse because he only understood the first few minutes, unless of course you speak his language. What! Men speak a different language? It might as well be if he doesn't understand you.

Men live in the now and future, that's why it's easy for (again, I am generally speaking) them to move on and feel after you had the talk it's over. When you bring it up again, they'll be like...I thought we were done with that.

Women speak from their feelings and are emotionally tied to the past. Women will bode well learning how to speak _____ (put your husband's name here).

The #1 thing a man wants to feel in his relationship is RESPECTED. The #1 thing a woman wants...communication and security. Yes, that was 2 things for women lol. Are men feeling beings? Of course, they are, but to get to those feelings or to hear yours they need adjectives.

When a woman says I feel you are not paying attention to me. You leave him to think (I texted her that I love her, I made coffee this morning, I said good morning) remember men are here now and future. The woman may mean two days ago you didn't acknowledge me when I said...or when you are looking at your cellphone for too long it makes me feel...

So, does that mean women think men should assume or be mind-readers? In most cases yes, women think men should know what they are feeling.

When a woman is quiet, she is usually mad or contemplating, when a man is quiet, he's thinking about football, golf, fishing or yeah food and sex. Is it that simple? Men are more like an on/off switch and women are like an airplane cockpit of switches, buttons and knobs.

Try to put your feelings into adjectives so he can understand what you are trying to communicate. Using the example above... yesterday, when you ignored me, it made me sad.

Men usually want to fix things. They need a beginning, middle and end. Understanding this difference between you and your husband will begin to set the stage of speaking each other's language.

Pray, Lord change me to better understand my husband. Help me to communicate with him, give him encouragement that he needs, help me to listen to understand him. I give you our marriage, you ordained it, let no man put it asunder. Amen!

Love...I'm in love, I'm so attracted to him, we've been married for so many years, I am falling out of love, I am falling in love... these are some of the things we say about love. Can you fall in love, then you can fall out of love, right?

Do you fall in love with your parents? No, you just love them for who they are and what they do for you, right?

Is love just a feeling or a choice? The Bible says love is kind, patient, gentle...are you towards your spouse or parents and children? Love does not dishonor, it is not easily angered, it does not keep records of wrong.

Do you throw in your spouse's face, all the records of every wrong from the past?

Love does not delight in evil but rejoices with the truth. 1 Corinthians 13:6

How did your love stack up to what the Bible says? Do you honor your husband, parents and yes, children?

Are you so angry with your husband that you silently rejoice when something goes wrong (evil) with him?

Do you lord over his shortcomings or past mistakes bringing it up every time like a bat to his head...well you did this or that...?

Love is gentle, love is kind, agape love; a God like love, is unconditional.

You do not fall out of love. It is a daily choice... It grows with each year that you are together. It matures into this comfortable love that you care so much for this person. You care about their health, mental health and happiness.

Some people treat their friends or strangers better then you treat your spouse or family.

Choose to be gentle, kind and respectful today in your partnership.

Yes, marriage is a partnership, you have finances to deal with, decisions to make about the marriage, planning...so like a business you are respecting your partners choices, you have meetings to discuss the plans and the future of your marriage. You set goals.

Coming together for the sole purpose of making the marriage work.

So then, love is a choice! I choose to be kind, I choose to honor, I choose my marriage.

After 20 years, I love my husband more today than when we 1st met. That feeling of falling in love, was just a feeling, today it's my choice and commitment to love him.

Pain changes people, hurt keeps you stuck and focused on your circumstances. Your thought process is all horizontal (concentrating on the problem).

Lift your pain up, lift your hurt up, lift your thoughts up and most importantly...lift your circumstances up to the Changer of your circumstances.

Focus on what He says, speak it out loud, change your perception... look up!

We were not meant to carry these burdens, they are too heavy. We are laden downwards with this heavy stuff. Look up and lighten your load...give it to Him today.

Father God I cannot carry this _____ (insert your troubles) any longer. Your word says your yoke is easy. I cast this _____ to You and trust that you will _____ (insert prosper me, give me health, help me). I ask you to forgive me of my part in this and I will praise you and give you all the glory. Thank You Lord for loving me, changing me and directing my path. In Jesus name.

Personal growth...if you don't take care of yourself, no one will.

Seek after growth, change your thoughts, the way you treat yourself, change your attitude towards yourself...it all starts with you.

Pray Lord change me! Women too often being the care takers and nurturer try to fix their spouse, their kids and their situation or they say "if only".

You are only responsible for what you say, your actions, and what you do.

If the other person is not willing, it is not up to you.

Only God can change a person's heart, but even God needs a willing participant.

Don't fall into the victim trap. With Christ Jesus you are victorious! But it takes applying God's word in your life. Follow His blueprint to peace and joy in your life.

If you are in a fix it-mode in a relationship...stop! Lord change me...allow God to work. Are you a willing participant?

You have not because you ask not. God tells us to lay our petitions before Him.

A petition is an exact legal document spelling out in detail what you are asking the courts for. Leave an item out and the court doesn't grant it in their judgment.

When we pray for something be specific in your prayer. I prayed for 12 years, yes that's right, 12 years with a list of what I wanted in a husband. #1 that he loves the Lord with all his heart. #2 he had a good sense of humor, and more. I had a list of the things I wanted and a list of absolute, drop-dead no's.

God presented to me 20 years ago a man with all the pros in my list. The things I failed to ask for guess what...I didn't get in him.

God's timing is in the blink of an eye for Him, but for me it was 12 years. Reconciliation of my marriage was 3.5 years. We don't see all the things in the spiritual realm that has to be worked out. It takes time, but God sees it as done!

When you lay your petitions before Him be careful what you ask for, know what you need and ask your Good Father who is waiting to talk (prayer) with you.

When I prayed for 12 years, he gave me a man who lived 8 hours away in NC.

All we had was conversation. We would talk on the phone every day for hours. He would drive 8 hours one-way to see me once a month. We became friends first. Long distance was all we had. But in these conversations, we got to know one another. When we grew closer, we discussed what we wanted in the marriage. We discussed finances, cleaning, raising kids...everything you can think of in a marriage, we discussed. It was awesome living long distance because God knew we needed that time to share and get to know one another without the flesh being involved.

If you are praying for a mate, be specific in your prayer. Write the pros and cons of the person you are praying for. Then keep the list and pray daily for this promised spouse. Use scripture on finding a spouse, love and marriage.

Ecclesiastes 4:9: "Two are better than one, because they have a good return for their labor: If either of them falls down, one can help the other up. But pity anyone who falls and has no one to help them up. Also, if two lies down together, they will keep warm. But how can one keep warm alone?"

Do premarital counseling to get all the ant hills that become mountains in a marriage out of the way. Yes, even if you've been married before, this is the best place to start once you begin talking marriage you want a plan. After all you both are going into this Covenant as partners and partners draw up a business plan (in this case a marriage plan).

Then watch God present to you your Adam or Eve. But ask Him, Lord if this is the one open the door wide. If not slam that door shut. He answers prayers!

There's so much noise coming at us every day. Do we really know how to be still before the Lord? Do you recognize His still small voice?

Just for a few minutes close your eyes, what do you hear? Cars passing by your house? Horns honking? People talking? The hum of your AC unit cooling your home? Do we really know what quiet sounds like?

When God speaks, it is not to your head, there is where either we speak to ourselves with thoughts of the day, past thoughts, or the enemy putting thoughts into your head.

Dwelling on these thoughts only grow into anxiety, criticism, confusion, doubt, fear or other negative thoughts. These are contrary to His word. God always confirms His word to you.

Can thoughts be positive? Absolutely if you train your mind to see through a different paradigm, one of encouragement, keeping all thoughts captive making them obedient to Christ.

There are so many kinds of voices in the world, and none of them is without signification...1 Corinthians 14:10

So how do I know the voice of the Lord? He says "I will put my laws into their mind, and write them in their hearts...Heb 8:10

His law comes from reading the Bible, knowing who He is, knowing His truths. Faith comes by hearing, knowing God.

Jn 10:3, 27...the sheep hear His voice and He calls His sheep by name, and He leads them out...my sheep hear and know My voice.

When the Lord speaks it is evident by an inward knowing, it always conforms to His word. He confirms, there is peace, trust, confidence, assurance and clarity.

Get to know God, spend time with Him, read the Bible, He wants relationship not prisoners. He wants to walk with you and talk with you...yes, along life's way (okay that's from an oldie but goodie hymn).

If you doubt, fear, have confusion, discomfort, question, no peace...it is not God. Satan may use the word god, but he will not call Jesus Christ Lord.

Let's talk about a subject that hurts, is so dark and sad that when it happens most people are surprised...suicide. Equally as difficult it is to talk about it, it is hard for me to write this.

For those who are left behind we ask how come we didn't know. Were there clues? Yeah, maybe you knew they were sad, but this...

Suicide for the person doesn't happen in a day (although the act of suicide does) the thoughts and contemplation could take years of depression and then finally hopelessness. It starts out like being thrown into a dark cold well, they can still look up and see the light. For them they have an internal struggle with these thoughts and they grow darker each time until they are in a rabbit hole and darkness is all they see. To them there is no hope and the relief is to end the struggle...the fight and pain.

Truly it is a permanent solution to a temporary problem, no matter how long the struggle; fight and fight you must.

Many of the greatest saints and heroes in the Bible faced overwhelming depression and sometimes wrote that they wished they had never even been born. King David, (Psalm 13:2-4), the prophet Jeremiah, (Jeremiah 20:14-18), and Job, (Job 7:15-16) among others, all reached low points where they despaired of their very lives. Job says, "So that my soul chooseth strangling, and death rather than my life. I loathe it; I would not live always: let me alone; for my days are vanity" (Job 7:15-16).

The struggle in their lives may show externally for a brief period; but many times, because no one wants to talk about this, they internalize it and then we are surprised. This internal dialogue you will never know is where the struggle (make forceful or violent efforts to get free of restraints or constraints) fight or wrestle goes on for sometimes years.

We need to get to them before the dark rabbit hole. For this is where they want to put an end to the struggle. When they are in the well, they too are fighting between life or death. In the rabbit hole...all they can see is relief in death. The morning doesn't bring light to them anymore, just more pain. Hope is gone and suicide is the answer for them.

If you are contemplating suicide, reach out! I know that you have in a way, maybe once or twice and perhaps no one took it seriously. Reach out again to someone who will!

For those left behind you have heard suicide is selfish but they are in such pain they cannot see anything or anyone else. The internal battle blinds them to any other emotions or people. We need to take every clue and verbal message they gave as a warning and help them see there is hope and a wonderful life past these dark thoughts.

Jesus is the only way! He says you can, but you will need help and the Hope of mankind. Spiritually suicide is the enemy's way of blinding you with hopelessness.

There is always hope, darkness is but for a night and in the morning does come the light. You need to get the help to crawl out of the well and see the Light of the World!

8 ways to get rid of anxiety:

1. Pray, mediate on the Word, and listen to praise and worship songs.
2. Journal-write your thoughts and positive things that happen throughout the day.
3. Talk-to godly women. Advice from the world will just give you worldly ways. You get enough of that. Get the Word inside you.
4. Clean up your food; get rid of sugar in your diet. Eat clean.
5. Name your feelings; too many of us don't know why we are sad, angry or depressed. Name it; there is a root cause to your sadness.
6. Breathe, yes breathe. In through your nose and out of your mouth, deep ones do like 3 times. Get oxygen to your brain. Do this many times throughout the day.

7. Exercise- move your body, take walks, just get up and do something. Don't seclude yourself.
8. Have an attitude of gratitude. Thank the Lord for another morning to do something different.

Your faith needs to be exercised; it needs to be used. His Word is a blueprint of how we should live our lives...follow it and find the Peace that surpasses all understanding!

Tools in Your Tool-Belt

The Pause – before reacting pause for a few seconds, take 3 deep cleansing breathes, in through your nose and out through your mouth

Setting healthy boundaries – do not allow others abuse, disrespect or to overstep the boundaries you created

Not everything requires an answer – Jesus was silent many times when confronted

Learn to let things go

Learn to forgive others and more importantly yourself

Give yourself grace and mercy, stop being so hard on yourself – if God can give you Grace and Mercy so can you

Learn more about yourself, your triggers, flags

Ask yourself; how, what, where, when and why. Find your root cause

Listen to understand, not respond or react

Ask clarifying questions, don't assume

Be in balance, mentally, spiritually, physically and emotionally

Make lists to stay organized

Begin journaling, write down your blessings

Make your conversations about win/win so no one leaves the conversation feeling unresolved lose/lose

Change your perspective

Shame keeps us imprisoned to a past event. The definition of shame is a painful feeling of humiliation or distress caused by the consciousness of wrong or foolish behavior. Read that again, it's a feeling...that feeling can keep you tied to that event for years. No one else may even know, just you, your past and it torments you to this day.

Listen, there is no one without sin, except for 1 man who walked on this earth over 2000 years ago. We all have a past, we can either learn from it, garner wisdom from those who have moved on and learn how to let go.

I have the secret sauce, the miracle cure...want to know how? Keep reading...

Everyday all that I write in here daily is the journey of healing and letting go. Discover the tools, discover yourself and immerse yourself in the Word of God daily.

He is your secret sauce...Jesus is our Miracle. He took on our shame, so we can give it to Him and be free.

I carried shame around for years. It was so heavy like a chain and 100lb weight around my neck for 23 years. Imagine what that does to a person, keeping shame locked away inside you for 23 years! It torments you; it replays in your mind again and again. You can delete it!

Like a line drawn in the sand, I felt if I crossed over the shame, if I let it out, that it would break me. The complete opposite was true. It was the letting it out to someone safe, a woman of God that I was able to let go of that tormenting spirit of shame. That shame morphs into depression and suicidal thoughts.

It didn't break me like I thought, it freed me...oh praise the name of Jesus...I am free.

You too can be free of bondage. You have the choice to hold onto it or be free of it. This day what do you choose?

Roman's 13:1-7 Let every person be subject to the governing authorities. For there is no authority except from God, and those that exist have been instituted by God. Therefore, whoever resists the authorities resists what God has appointed, and those who resist will incur judgment. For rulers are not a terror to good conduct, but too bad. Would you have no fear of the one who is in authority? Then do what is good, and you will receive his approval, for he is God's servant for your good. But if you do wrong, be afraid, for he does not bear the sword in vain. For he is the servant of God, an avenger who carries out God's wrath on the wrongdoer. Therefore, one must be in subjection, not only to avoid God's wrath but also for the sake of conscience...

No matter which way things turn out, we must pray that God is victorious.

I see posts that say you can't hate and be a Christian. This is an incredible misleading statement. Rather it should say you can't hate and be in a relationship with Jesus.

It is religion and old testament ways, putting God in a box kind of thinking.

I am a Christian, what does that mean to me? I have the Spirit of the Living Lord on the inside of me. His heart is my heart, it's a relationship with Him who sticks closer than a friend. He never leaves me or forsakes me.

I fall short of the Glory of God, my sin is as filthy rags, BUT He loves me through it and like a Loving Father, welcomes me back into His Arms every time I pray and ask forgiveness.

I am not religious; I am a child of God!

If we have the choice to speak positive instead of negative, to choose joy and peace, then we have the choice to learn that our past is a learning experience and it only defines us...if and what we let it.

I am a failure, if you quit trying...learn from it and grow past it.

I have no money...are you a good steward over what you do have? What can you do to increase your income? Or decrease your bills? Choices!

We make daily decisions some out of habit, without realizing them. If we are intentional about our decisions and choices, we can make changes then for the better. Understanding ourselves is the 1st step.

Without change growth is impossible. Staying the same day in and day out; only you can make the decision to grow through it.

Open the eyes of my heart Lord, help me to make the right choices to leave the broken pieces and allow you to sew me back together again. Give me beauty for my ashes, joy for my sorrows and replace in me what needs to go in Jesus's name.

What choices will you make today? To make your bed, or not? To shower, to have a cup of coffee, or to exercise?

What about the choice to have joy, laughter or to be positive? Can you choose these things? Yes, of course, you have the power to choose positive over negative thoughts. You have the choice to plan out your day or just take it as it comes.

Joshua 24:15 choose for yourselves this day whom you will serve...

I choose the Lord and all His promises and blessings.

Think positive, speak positive and be positive...

I am That I am. What does that mean? I believe it means different things to different people. To me, it was our Creator saying, He is to us what we need Him to be at a moment in time.

When we are sad, He is our Joy.

When we are out of sorts, He is our Peace.

When we are depressed, He is our Comforter.

When we are sick, He is our Healer.

When we are alone, He is closer than any friend.

When we don't know how we are going to eat, He is our Provider.

When we need medicine, He is our Doctor.

When we are in a legal battle, He is our Counselor.

The Great I Am, is what You need Him to be right now!

Jesus, great "I AM" and Lord of what is, said, "Come to me, all you who are weary and burdened, and I will give you rest." (Matthew 11:28).

I am what He says I am! With so many voices out there tearing us down, remember who you are in Christ Jesus.

Below are quotes from excerpts from Bible Reasons:

"My deepest awareness of myself is that I am deeply loved by Jesus Christ and I have done nothing to earn it or deserve it."

"Our true identity is found when we stop being "who we are" and start being who we were created to be."

"I am a daughter of the King, who is not moved by the world. For my God is with me and goes before me. I do not fear because I am His."

"The more you reaffirm who you are in Christ, the more your behavior will begin to reflect your true identity."

Start speaking positivity over you and your life. I am a child of God!

This overwhelming feeling of doom and gloom is just too much to bear. Each day I wake up to repeat the day before, it doesn't seem to get better; but worse.

This world isn't helping either, the human suffering is too much for my soul to bear. Who hates who, people are so mean and rude to one another, is there anyone who can speak calmly or nice?

The news doesn't speak the truth, our government has become too involved in our lives, mandates, executive orders, wearing masks, our children are suffering. Going out and socially distancing is making everyone suspicious and downright rude. We have become isolated and human contact is being erased.

God made us to interact with each other. He said it was not good for man to be alone.

We were born for such a time as this. God needs vessels to prepare others for disciples. We are in Revelations, nightmares, visions and dreams. Moral abominations, sound familiar?

Revelation 21 Then I saw a new heaven and a new earth, for the first heaven and the first earth had passed away, and there was no longer any sea. I saw the Holy City, the new Jerusalem, coming down out of heaven from God, prepared as a bride beautifully dressed for her husband.

Revelation 3:20 Here I am! I stand at the door and knock. If anyone hears my voice and opens the door, I will come in and eat with them, and they with me.

Do you hear Him knocking? People get ready!

Do you trust God? Or do you pray more, harder and plea to Him to move on your behalf?

He doesn't want you to try harder, He wants your trust, your faith!

We don't pray back God's word to remind Him of His promises, we pray it back to build our faith and remind us that His word is Yes and Amen.

He doesn't want us begging, but to believe that when we ask Him then we begin thanking Him with expectation of answered prayer.

Then why did I pray for 12 years for my husband? Couldn't God have presented him in an instant? Remember God is Spirit, we are natural. His timing is not measured in seconds or minutes. A thousand years to us is a blink of His time; it's perfect!

During that 12 years He was preparing my husband for me. Teaching him and me lessons, getting us both ready for one another. Then at the right occasion (Leo in NC and I in NJ) God presented us to one another.

It would have been (either one of us) free will to not have chosen the other. That is not to say in the 12 years men or women weren't presented to either of us. There were many; the enemy even tempted with some. But I prayed with each one Lord, if he is not your will, slam that door shut. And that He did!

I pray for all decisions in my life, I want His will, if it's not of God, I don't want it.

Whatever you are praying for trust, have faith, see with spiritual eyes and begin thanking Him that it is yours in Jesus's name!

I went past the field of the sluggard...the ground was covered with weeds and the stone wall was in ruins...Proverbs 24:30

What is your work ethic like? Are you determined to get the job done? God says, he who is slothful in his work, is a brother to...a great destroyer...Proverbs 18:9

Or are you a procrastinator? I'll do it tomorrow, but your projects lay in 1/2 completed state, if started at all. Half built, half painted, untidy garage...the list goes on.

A master of excuses, so many reasons not to fulfill the job. Do you?

Get up, make the bed, get dressed, show up, work as unto the Lord.

Laziness produces lack, the thief will rob you. Those who complain, cut corners, cripple businesses, cause hardships.

Go to your job today thankful that you have a job. Do the job with an attitude of gratitude. Succeed at your job, succeed at life, your marriage, relationships and your relationship with God.

Today, Lord Jesus, I give you honor and Glory for my job. Prosper my place of business, expand my territory. Thank you for my job. You are awesome in my life! Amen

Living life in balance, too much of anything is not good for us. Ice cream is tasty, too much of it is not good for us. Why even water is a necessity to live, too much of it is not.

Sadness is a live emotion, it signals us to the reality of something, too much can lead us to depression. The bible says in Proverbs 23:30 do not crave his delicacies, for that food is deceptive.

Living life in balance; mind (mental), body (physical), and spirit is the key to a happy life. Balance a distribution of weight (in this case mind, body and spirit) enabling someone to remain upright and steady.

Listen, we all fall short of the Glory of God; the answer is to recognize it when you are out of balance quickly and get back into balance.

The enemy knows you better than you do. We all need to know and understand ourselves, mind, body and spirit so that when he comes in like a flood, we look to the One who can stop him.

Managing your stress. Learning to live interoceptive. Stress is the sense of the internal state of the body. Our brain processing signals related from our body to specific sub regions. Sense helps us to understand and feel what is going on inside our body.

So, if we can sense when we are cold or hot, then we can sense when we are stressed. But often we over look this one sense and keep on working or doing that same thing that is stressful.

Being mindful of our internal signal that is telling us to rest. God created 1 day of rest. How do you take it? Mowing the lawn, shopping for food?

When we finally do rest, we get anxious or panic attacks from doing too much.

We need to stop, pray, rest our mind, spirit, breathe, exhale and exercise this vessel that God gave you.

Learning to live inside out gives us a whole new perspective on life. What is important. Thriving not surviving!

Rest does not mean just doing nothing. Resting your mind from TV, social media, busyness of "I have to do".

Taking your mind off the things of this world, immersing yourself in praise or worship or the things of God...this will quench your thirst and give you rest!

Do you know why you are feeling a certain way? The WHY is important to explore, it leads you to other emotions and then to the root of the feeling.

Did you know boredom can lead to many other emotions? Such as:

Weariness, lack of enthusiasm, lack of interest, lack of concern, apathy, interestedness, unconcern, languor, sluggishness, frustration, dissatisfaction, restlessness, tediousness, dullness, monotony, repetitiveness, lack of variety, lack of variation, flatness, blandness, sameness, uniformity, routine, humdrum, dreariness, lack of excitement. Just the words above make you emotionless.

The person can exhibit withdrawal, become quiet or the opposite, restless, or angry. But once they dig deep, they find out the why.

We need to become emotionally mature, intelligent that when we are acting out, there is always a why.

If we don't, we are in danger of it morphing into other issues. The feeling can exhibit other types of behaviors as well.

Get to know your feelings, don't be afraid of them. They will help you discover why am I feeling this way, then you can take corrective measures to resolving it.

There is always a primary, secondary and tertiary emotions. Love-primary, affection, lust, longing-secondary and adoration, desire, longing-tertiary.

Anger-primary
Irritation, rage, disgust, envy-secondary
Annoyed, grouchiness, grumpy-tertiary.

You see there is always a why with our emotions. Once you conquer this there is healing on the other side. Listen like surgery you are cut, bleed and then sewn back up. It takes time to heal. Give yourself the grace to feel, but don't get stuck.

Remember with Christ Jesus you can do this, His yoke is easy!

Perspective what is yours like today? If you change yours, you can change your way of thinking. Really, if I change a particular attitude towards or regarding something, I can see it differently? Yes!

Have you ever looked at a picture and there is something else to see? Like there is something else in the picture and when you look real-close you see it. It now becomes something else. Our attitudes and mind are strong and gives us a false sense of things. Can we trust what we see? Not always.

If we change our lens of how we are viewing a situation, pause, breathe, exhale and put on our spiritual glasses and look through the lens of our heart, love and see it differently we can change the situation.

He will take your mess and turn it into a message. He will take your pain and turn it into something beautiful. He will take every fiery dart and they shall not prosper. He will take what others meant for harm and use it for the good of His people.

What does He want from you? Your trust, your faith, and belief that when you pray with expectation that it is already done in Jesus's name!

The definition of perspective: a particular attitude toward or way of regarding something; a point of view.

Change your thoughts, renew your mind and change your heart. Renewing your mind is the only way you can experience change. Old thinking gives you old ways.

Recently I posted a picture of a black rug, those who saw the black Labrador will never see the rug the same. They will always see the dog too.

What do you see in the picture below? Once you see it differently, you can't continue to see it the same way. With the renewing of our minds, we change our perspective.

Let God transform you into a new person by changing the way you think. Roman's 12:2

I want change, I want growth...I don't want to stay stuck and wandering in darkness. I want what Jesus says I am.

I surrender my will to Him and I want what He has for me. Are you ready to let go of your past hurts? Hasn't it consumed you long enough?

God will restore what the locus has stolen. Let Him give you beauty for ashes.

Our words carry the force of a strong offensive or retaliatory blow. It can be as strong as someone punching you in the chest and knocking the wind out of you. Have you ever had the wind knocked out of you? I have, you are doubled over in pain, grasping for breath, but you can't catch it. It hurts!

Your words yes, the ones that come out of your mouth has the same power to serve up that force blow, to knock someone off just with what is coming out of our mouth. What are you using yours for? To build up (life) encouragement? Or always tearing down (death)?

Abuse can be verbal and it delivers a strike force that goes deep inside the persons soul. A bruise heals and the pain goes away but those words you continue to hit that person with, is rooted deep inside them. This pain of yours will take years of therapy and healing just because of what you have spoken over them. I know what I say because I have lived abuse, sexually, emotionally, physically and verbally for years. And it has taken me years of healing to be who I am today.

When you live for years and years with being told: you're ugly, you're not good enough, you'll never amount to anything, people will never like you, you're stupid, you can't do anything right, you're not smart, no one likes you, no one loves you...guess what happens you become what has been served with their barrage of words...you become those things! I walked around wounded for years thinking I was unlovable, stupid and I would never amount to anything.

One negative word can tear down 100 positive words spoken. Read that again please, yes 1 negative word. You think while you say to your husband you don't feel, you're not sensitive, you don't know how to love; that it doesn't hurt him? That those words don't go to his very soul? He becomes what you say. You constantly say about your child, he's a monster, the devil child he starts acting just like you speak over him, rowdy and uncontrollable.

STOP! Your words are powerful! They can soothe, give life or death. What my little words...YES! They are containers of power. Start flowing from your mouth words of edification, speak life into your spouse and children. Pray blessing over them. What do you want in him? Speak it to him. You are kind, loving, gentle, you show me love in the most special ways. You get what you pour in.

Want your children to stop acting like monsters? Tell them how good they are, special, God's gift, they are going to amount to wonderful children of God. Just watch how quickly your words can tear down and how much longer to build up. What do you choose to do today? I choose to edify, encourage, speak life, put smiles on faces, let people know they can do it and go through it with Christ Jesus who strengthens us. We can! We are strong! We can endure! We are victorious! We are loved!

I am not weak, I am loved, I am beautiful, I am blessed, I am strong, I am the daughter of ABBA Father nothing is too difficult for Him. I Am A Child of God. I am not a slave to fear, to what has been spoken over me. Those chains have been broken and I am free! Praise God He is Mighty to Save! Today, let no negative hurtful words depart from your lips. Speak life into everyone you come in contact with. Start today and change those around you. You have what you say. What say you?

My trust is broken, he has betrayed me, I can never trust again. He has hurt me so bad; can I ever love again?

I feel so lost, depressed unwanted, I'm not worthy of anyone. I don't even feel like a person, I rather feel like a piece of rag. I am nothing, no one...oh God help me. If you are real show yourself to me, help me through this painful phase of my life. I can't breathe it hurts so bad.

But Your word says I am your chosen one, you say I am worthy, you call me beautiful the apple of your eye. You say I am valuable, help me to be a vessel You can work through. My Father, Advocate, Counselor, my Peace, my Joy. The One who will never leave me or forsake me.

I cast this burden to you. It is too heavy for me to carry. I am free from drugs, drinking, I am free from gluttony, I am free from tormenting spirits, in Jesus's name I am free! Enemy you are beneath my feet. You have no authority over me. I am a child of God. Hallelujah!

This is how we fight! Prayer, Spirit-filled, and in Jesus's name. Breaking down strongholds.

MATTHEW 11:30 For my yoke is easy, and my burden is light.

We were not meant to carry our burdens. They weigh us down. Imagine every burden as a 25lb weight of poundage of rocks that we carry around on our backs and necks.

Would we be able to stand upright? I think not, we would all recognize each other by our slumped over stances...wow they really have a lot of burdens, look how bent over he/she is!

We are to cast our burdens to Him, give them to Him and watch each care that we carry be lifted off us and onto the Lifter of our heads.

Imagine a mother is carrying a baby, diaper bag, having to do the dishes, laundry, clean the house, do the shopping and work a full-time job...look at the weight of it all. Cast them off one by one and DON'T take them back and watch God move on your behalf. Those who wait upon the Lord will see His Hand move!

What is weighing you down today? What can you lay down at His Feet and carry it no more? Will you? Don't pick it back up, trust Him and have faith that He can do all things!

Darkness covers and the light reveals. Ever notice how much is hidden in darkness? Just a flicker of a candle and the darkness dissipates. Bring out a flashlight and it withdraws from where you shine the light. Most birds quiet down and stop flying in the night. For nocturnal animals, the darkness is their time to hunt. Under the cover of darkness much is hidden.

What is it that you are hiding? What is it that you don't want revealed? What is it that you are keeping covered? Staying hidden won't change things. It festers, it goes deep into your being and things don't ad won't get better; it grows and we get sicker.

It's when you shine a light into those deep dark wounds and finally say enough is enough, I want to heal, I want to get better, I need to change; He will be there for you when everyone else has failed you.

Weeping may endure for a night, but joy comes in the morning. However long the night is, morning always comes.

What is it that you are still hiding? Like a cut, it has to bleed, ooze, scab over to heal. His grace is sufficient, it protects, secures and calms...gives you peace.

By talking to a woman of God, who will give you back the word of God, He will make your path straight. You can and will get through the darkness by His strength. He is the God of comfort.

Are you ready to lay it all at His feet? Let His light shine into all your dark places.

Lord help me with _____ (name it). I need to give it to you. Your yoke is easy, this is too heavy of a burden for me to carry.

I invite Your Spirit of peace, love and kindness into the dark rooms of my being, to shine the Holy Spirit flashlight on all the things that I need to lay at your feet. I declare healing from my past. I pray with expectation for your word does not return void. I am healed in Jesus's name!

Let's talk about healing. If I can only touch the hem of His garment...

What does that say to you? She believed beyond a shadow of doubt that was all she needed to do...touch His hem and she would be healed.

Jesus knew someone touched Him. With thousands of people pressing in from all sides, He knew His hem (power) went out of Him.

By her faith, belief, her unwavering, I know, that I know, I will be healed and she was.

When you pray, do you doubt? Or do you pray beyond a shadow of doubt you know He hears you and He heals, He answers prayers?

When we pray back God's word, it's not for Him, He knows His word. It's for us to build our faith, that we know His word does NOT return void (empty).

Stop looking horizontal (at your circumstances) and look up to your God who created all things and know He is mighty to save! Do you believe? Is your faith...if I just touch His hem, I'll be healed?

Today, pray with all your heart, all your mind, all your faith and ask Jesus to heal you.

The thief comes quietly, he's sneaky, and under the cover of darkness he attacks...out of seemingly nowhere.

Have you ever watched a video of a thief checking car doors, he's dressed in black, covers his head, wears a hoodie or baseball cap so you can't identify him?

So is our enemy crawling on his belly to sneak up on us, to pop up when you least expect it. He knows us well! Put on the full armor of God so you are well protected. When he attacks you are able to withstand the barrage of fiery darts aimed at you.

When they come and come, they will...your response is not to cry, sulk, scream or yell but to STAND and say not today Satan, but my God is bigger than this!

Cry out to ABBA Father and let Him send His warrior Angel's to surround you. When you are surrounded by the ups and downs of life...God's got this! We serve an awesome God.

We are all born with a God given void. When we were born there is an emptiness, a longing placed in our hearts.

A void means; empty completely vacant, without contents, containing nothing, blank, bare, unfilled, unoccupied, uninhabited, a desolate gap, an empty space.

What are you filling your void up with? Drugs, alcohol, pornography...these are gap fillers. They will not provide you the God plug for this empty void.

Only God can plug it up. He created it in you so you would search for Him.

Not even your friends or spouse can fill this empty space. That is why man will always disappoint but our Lord and Savior will always fill your void.

It is no wonder we search our whole life for the meaning of life, someone, something to fulfill us; when it is only Jesus and His Holy Spirit. That once we are filled with the Holy Spirit are, we full.

So, come Holy Spirit and fill us with your love, mercy, compassion, grace and forgive us this day.

Victory is born out of struggle. It is where we learn. We learn from our pain. Don't be afraid of it, face it, it's where you will grow.

Ruth, Naomi and Oprah experienced a unique bonding because of their experiences, like a support group. You can't learn from someone who hasn't walked in your shoes. People can't give you what they don't have. You forge great relationships from that bond.

Once you start to make sense of your pain, a support group can help you sort through it, with other women or men that have walked it.

When God begins to bless you remember who gave you the overabundance. Thank Him for the small and big things.

Life is for the living, get back into it. Give Him back the wheel, there is no better Driver!

The Holy Spirit is relentless. Have you ever had Him urge you to do something or say something to someone? It will feel like a pushing in your spirit to speak up. It won't last forever and if you aren't obedient, He will move on to find a willing vessel.

Many times, in church seated in my seat a person next to me, a total stranger...the Holy Spirit will tell me to say this___ to them. I struggle with my humanness and wait. The Holy Spirit has a Rama word for them, life changing and I struggle with my humanness.

But finally, I turn to this stranger and say exactly what the Holy Spirit has for them and BAM...transformation begins.

It's not about us, it is all about Him. He is Spirit and needs His people to work through. It is not gloating or being haughty, it is a humbling experience. It is an honor to be used by Him.

Then, once in a while this total stranger will tell you that the word you gave them was the seed that they needed to burst in them their journey of walking with the Lord. The Holy Spirit now has another vessel to work through. Oh hallelujah, it's not about me, it's all about You Jesus!

We are what we learn. We are all a product of our environment and our parent's teachings. Everyone we come in contact with influences us in one way or another. Who or what is influencing you today?

Just like we are what we eat...eat donuts and sugar all the time the evidence will show itself in your belly and on your hips.

Eat clean and exercise, well you get where I am going here. We are not just body; we have a mind that has been developing since birth.

Our Creator made us to be thinking, feeling and spiritual beings. What are you feeding or filling yourself up with?

God's word is our blueprint of how we should live. If something is not right in your life...go to the word! It will give you the answer which way to turn. It is always to God; His yoke is easy. We were not created to carry such heavy burdens.

The word is filled with God's promises and answers. If we all can come out of our feelings and go into our spiritual self-quicker, we would save ourselves from a lot of pain and grief.

As for me and my house I shall serve the Lord. When those fiery dart are aimed at you, call out God's word that they shall not prosper. Be so filled with His scriptures that they pour out of your mouth while you stand!

Praise Jesus that He my Advocate, my Counselor, my Peace, thank you Father that you watch over me, keep me safe from my enemies. What they mean for harm you shall turn it for the good of your people. Amen

We cry and it's good let the tears out. It's our bodies way of letting out the grief or pain we feel when there are no words.

When we isolate...this is when you need to reach out to someone. Isolation leads us to depression and hopelessness. There's nothing here but darkness...get out of this phase quickly.

When we get stuck...we can't move past the pain. This is when our emotions are tied to our pain. Acknowledge the emotion, name it and ask yourself questions about what and why you are feeling this way. Begin journaling, ask yourself exactly what or who has hurt you? Ask yourself why does this hurt so much?

Getting to the root of the pain will help you get past the pain. Asking yourself questions and journaling will begin the road to healing.

It will help you take ownership of your role in the situation. Be truthful when journaling, its painful to see yourself in a situation gone wrong, but it cannot be all the other person.

What did you do to either escalate it or begin it? Are you angry? Why are you angry? What did you say or do? Do you keep bringing up the past hurts? (You are stuck if you can't get past it, or it's just too new) wounds needs time to heal.

Be patient with yourself! The healing journey is a long one. But one that must be taken in order to get past it.

Be refreshed today, by the renewing of your mind daily...there is grace, there is hope...there is healing on the other side. His yoke is easy, we were not meant to carry these heavy burdens.

Are you ready to cast them aside? Are you packed and ready for this healing journey? There is joy, peace and love again!

We measure ourselves to one another and compare ourselves with one another without understanding, I wish I had her body, money, looks _____ you put it here.

STOP! Look your best, but accept what you can't change. God doesn't make mistakes. People Judge our outward appearance; God judges our hearts.

Start appreciating yourself! I am going to be 64 years old, a grandmother of 2 grandsons and have 2 beautiful daughters whom I am so proud of both of them. I have a husband who loves me no matter what. I am not at the weight I would like to be; but I try to look my best no matter. I am a blessed woman. I am counting my blessings, not my downfalls.

I am a child of the God most High. He loves me and He love you.

What season are you in? Just like the changes of winter, spring, summer and fall we go through seasons. Some of us get stuck in one and we don't move forward.

What has you stuck today? Is it something that happened years ago? If you don't deal with it like a tree with deep roots it will just keep growing.

Sure, you can hack at the leaves, but you will never get to the root.

Anger, depression, sadness and so on all have a root cause...find it and pull it out by the roots and it will grow no more.

How do you do it? If you are 50 years old and this root happened when you were 20, you've been carrying it for 30 years. It's going to take a healing journey to uncover it, talk about it and go through the process of healing.

It's not quick and easy but when you take the healing journey...oh at the end comes joy, lightness and freedom!

Find the help you need, reach out, let God help you through it. He is waiting with "out stretched arms".

No one can do the healing for you, it takes your application of what you learn and working the journey of your healing.

There is freedom, joy and peace!

Where do you see yourself in 1 year? 5 years? How do you plan to achieve these goals? Did you write them down on paper, or just think about them?

Something happens when you take pen to paper and write them down. Same as speaking them out loud. They become real, rather than just thoughts or dreams.

Making deliberate choices to get you towards that goal is only 1 step. Always take it to God 1st, because if it's not His Will for my life, I don't want it.

He knows and already has a plan for you, a plan to prosper you. Your destiny is in His Hands. I want that!

Holy Spirit fill this vessel with your plans for me to fulfill my destiny. Lord Jesus make me a vessel that you can use. When I enter those Gates, I want to hear well done my good and faithful servant.

Are you an enabler? A person or thing that makes something possible. A person who encourages or enables negative or self-destructive behavior in another.

We do it without even knowing or realizing the harm or codependency we create in the person or situation. We think we are helping or loving, but don't realize we are handicapping the person. We take away their decision-making by making it for them or just taking control and getting it done.

Step away for a moment and try to see it from another perspective. What handcuffs have you put on the person by taking control? What blindfold have you put over their ability to see? How has it cut them off at the knees because you keep stepping in?

Whether it is your children, spouse or a situation...step back, pause and ask yourself if I... _____ will they?

Is it time to stop drinking milk and start eating solid food? The Lord wants us to grow up. Luke 2:40 And the child grew and became strong, filled with wisdom. And the favor of God was upon him.

Ask the Lord for wisdom.

Are you a right fighter? A do what's good person?

Galatians 6:9 Let us not lose heart in doing good, for in due time we will reap if we do not grow weary.

Psalm 103:6 The Lord performs righteous deeds and judgments for all who are oppressed.

Deuteronomy 32:4 "The Rock! His work is perfect, for all His ways are just; A God of faithfulness and without injustice, Righteous and upright are His.

God fights for us righteous and upright are His. Judgments are His and He frees to the oppressed.

We sometimes think we have to do it all, but He calls us to Peace that surpasses all understanding...His Peace, His Righteousness, His Will and not ours.

Total surrender to a King, a Father, a Lord and Savior who in return gives you Love, Joy, Peace, Grace and Mercy.

He will be a Righteous God, surrender your will to His, in Him is freedom for us.

Go ahead get rid of those weights, give them to Him, His yoke is easy, our burdens to great.

Teach them while they are young and when they grow old, they will not depart far from the word. Proverbs 22:6

Or another translation; Teach children how they should live, and they will remember it all their life. Different meaning?

We are what we learn, we didn't pick or choose our parents but God knew you in your mother's womb. Some of us have had the gift of awesome parents, some of us not so much. Some have life so easy and some struggle every day to survive.

God didn't promise us a rose garden, but He does say; keep His ways and He will stick closer to you than any friend.

Why is it life seems so easy for some, while other fight to eat? To this I know not the answer.

However, I do know I will never go hungry because He is my Provider. Put Him first in all things and He will make your paths straight. How do you put God first? Prayer the most powerful weapon in your arsenal!

How different my life would have been if I wasn't abused when I was young, didn't grow up poor and wasn't made fun of, no...it all made me into the woman I am today. God didn't waste a thing, He made me a warrior, strong, bold and my foundation built on Solid Rock.

When I wake up the enemy says, oh no she's awake because he knows who I serve. Thank you, my Jesus, without You I would not be where I am today. Praise Your Holy name.

Always asking yourself why or what leads you down a self-check path. It's not always the enemy or someone (thing) else. Sometimes it is us; we do it to ourselves.

Unresolved issues, thoughts or feelings can bring us back a year ago, 5 years ago or even more. Unresolved means simply something not finished/resolved.

It needs you to solve it. How do you do that? Ask yourself questions and like the root of a weed you don't want growing back again, you pluck it out by resolving it.

I was born, like everyone one day conceived in my mother's womb. I had no choices of what I would look like, the color of my skin, hair or eyes. It was all predetermined through my father and mother's genes. I had no choice of who my parents were either. They made a choice, that made me, just like you.

My outer shell may look different from you, but we all descend from the same Creator. His word says He knew us in our mother's womb, that none of us are a mistake. We were born for a time such as this, this generation, this moment; there's a reason.

God does not judge our outer shell, but our hearts. We all have emotions and only the Lord can judge our hearts.

When someone looks different, we treat them differently, from bullying to shaming and more; but God sees our hearts, all He sees is the truth, the real you.

Oh, to be so intimately known by our Father. We can't hide from Him; He sees all and knows all and still...He loves us. Like a loving parent, we can do wrong but with open arms He forgives.

How forgiving are you? Set yourself free, let go of the resentments, let go of the past and begin living life with letting go!

What are you holding onto today? Is it something that happened years ago? When you think about it, years later can you still see it, feel the pain and you get sick or angry from the memories?

Even though it happened 5-10 years ago the pain is as if it just happened. You get mad or want answers regarding a past circumstance. When you speak about it to someone the awful feelings come flooding back and it is as if it happened all over again.

Forgiveness true forgiveness is when you stop thinking, feeling or even speaking about it because you let it go...it no longer has a hold on you...you forgave!

Forgiveness is a gift to you, my friend. You don't need to like or love the perpetrator, or for that matter even speak with them, but in yourself you have to lay it at the feet of the cross and let it go. Isaiah 43:18 forget the former things, do not dwell on the past.

Our bodies have muscle memory too, our bodies can conjure up the pain it felt. It is not just the brain memories. Roses have thorns and unfortunately human relationships comes with hurts. Man will always disappoint, but your God will never fail you.

So today forgive, truly let go of what has you bound to the past. Let it go, do what you've been called to do and watch God move on your behalf.

What does it mean to be in the flesh? Giving in to temptations? Crying? Feeling sad, depressed, or allowing our emotions to run away with every thought? We are human right? We want to scream, yell, cry, bust out and just go with it when times of trouble come and they will come.

We are in this world, we live and breathe, when the shock of a situation or diagnosis comes our natural flesh feels it. Our natural mind starts with oh my, what about this...if that happens...this is going to happen or I'll have to do this and on and on. We make the situation worse in our minds and flesh.

Then we go and tell a friend or family member or worse post it on social media and now it's even larger than it was.

People thinking, they are helping give you advise, opinions and sometimes confusion now sets in and you are worse than when you got the news.

That is being in the flesh allowing your natural self to take the wheel. Nothing wrong with feelings, God made us that way.

But we are not of this world, we are to live spiritually. Let's take the same situation as above but now we are doing it God's way.

We get a diagnosis or bad news...we go straight to God. We tell no one except our spouse (if you have one) if not, a spiritual woman of God to pray with us. We play worship music, we cry out to ABBA Father, we straighten our crowns, stand boldly on His words and confess Jesus Christ is Lord. We pray!

We break every stronghold, we curse the root in Jesus' name, that sickness cannot take hold, we confess the diagnosis is wrong, that we believe the report of the Lord.

We are spirit so we fight and stand in the spirit, and boldly enter the throne room and come before our Father in Jesus name believing that He is able, that He is the Healer... oh come on...give Him the Glory. Have the faith of a mustard seed and watch Him move that mountain!

Judge not lest you be judged. Leave this up to the Lord for it is His to do.

Exodus 23:1-2 "Do not spread false reports. Do not help a guilty person by being a malicious witness. Do not follow the crowd in doing wrong. When you give testimony in a lawsuit, do not pervert justice by siding with the crowd and do not show favoritism to a poor person in a lawsuit.

Exodus 23:6-7 "Do not deny justice to your poor people in their lawsuits. Have nothing to do with a false charge and do not put an innocent or honest person to death, for I will not acquit the guilty.

Simply put it is not ours to judge.

You will get past this, like the snow, grief melts away. Over time it goes, but like winter the snow comes and the grief makes a reappearance. Sometimes it's an avalanche and smothers you. As time passes it does melt away.

We are meant to feel pain. Like a barometer, it alerts us that something is wrong. It helps us to pinpoint the area of hurt. If you go to a doctor, he will turn that area of pain and ask "does this hurt"?

Getting to your root cause of the pain will help you through the journey of healing. If you don't get to the why, it will keep rising up again.

Healing takes time, your body requires the time to properly heal. You can't rush the healing process.

You go to a doctor, physical therapist and or turn to other methods to heal a broken leg...don't try to heal the hidden pain.

Turn to the Healer of all your pain and don't attempt to do it on your own. Seek out the help you need. You don't need to suffer alone.

Are you ready to reach out? Are you ready to peel back the layers of hurt and begin to heal?

He promises, I will heal all your wounds!

You are only in control of you. You cannot control others, only your reaction, the words that come out of your mouth and what you do next.

Don't respond out of emotions. Don't make decisions out of feelings, pause, breathe...inhale deeply and exhale. Pray for His guidance daily.

Respond out of emotional Intelligence and emotional maturity, not out of past hurts or feelings. Remember women are emotionally tied to past hurts.

If you cannot get past these former wounds, reach out for help. Just like a wound it has to bleed, scab and then heal.

Don't you want joy, peace and love back in your heart? It can be done, but 1st you have to go through the fire to be refined.

Healing is yours; it starts 1st with a baby step of reaching out. Don't isolate yourself, that leads to depression. May you take that courageous leap today.

The definition of perspective: a particular attitude toward or way of regarding something; a point of view.

Change your thoughts, renew your mind and change your heart. Renewing your mind is the only way you can experience change. Old thinking gives you old ways.

It is with the renewing of our minds, that we change our perspective.

Let God transform you into a new person by changing the way you think. Roman's 12:2 NIV says "Do not conform to the pattern of this world, but be transformed by the renewing of your mind. Then you will be able to test and approve what God's will is — his good, pleasing and perfect will." ... Then you will learn to know God's will for you, which is good and pleasing and perfect."

I want change, I want growth...I don't want to stay stuck and wandering in darkness. I want what Jesus says I am.

I surrender my will to Him and I want what He has for me. Are you ready to let go of your past hurts? Hasn't it consumed you long enough?

God will restore what the locus has stolen. Let Him give you beauty for ashes.

Ephesians 6:11 (below 12-17): "Put on the whole armor of God, that you may be able to stand against the wiles (lies, deceit, trickery) of the devil."

We all have flight or fight tendencies. Which are you? Fight like a warrior of God? His weapons are not carnal; to fight like a warrior of God, is to PRAY in the spirit. Go before Him and use the language He poured down from heaven onto your tongue.

12 For our struggle is not against flesh and blood, but against the rulers, against the authorities, against the powers of this dark world and against the spiritual forces of evil in the heavenly realms.13 Therefore put on the full armor of God, so that when the day of evil comes, you may be able to stand your ground, and after you have done everything, to stand. 14 Stand firm then, with the belt of truth buckled around your waist, with the breastplate of righteousness in place, 15 and with your feet fitted with the readiness that comes from the gospel of peace.16 In addition to all this, take up the shield of faith, with which you can extinguish all the flaming arrows of the evil one. 17 Take the helmet of salvation and the sword of the Spirit, which is the word of God.

Ready your feet, carry that shield, put on the belt of TRUTH. He is looking for warriors...are you ready?

We cry and it's good let the tears out. It's our bodies way of letting out the grief or pain we feel when there are no words.

We isolate...this is when you need to reach out to someone. Isolation leads us to depression and hopelessness. There's nothing here but darkness...get out of this phase quickly.

We get stuck...we can't move past the pain. This is when our emotions are tied to our pain. Acknowledge it, ask yourself questions about what and why you are feeling this way. Begin journaling, ask yourself exactly what or who has hurt you? Ask yourself why does this hurt so much?

Getting to the root of the pain will help you get past the pain. Asking yourself questions and journaling will begin the road to healing.

It will help you take ownership of your role in the situation. Be truthful when journaling, it is painful to see yourself in a situation gone wrong, but it cannot be all the other person.

What did you do to either escalate it or begin it? Are you angry? Why are you angry? What did you say or do? Do you keep bringing up the past hurts? (You are stuck if you can't get past it, or it's just too new) wounds needs time to heal.

Be patient with yourself! The healing journey is a long one. But one that must be taken in order to get past it.

Be refreshed today, by the renewing of your mind daily...there is grace, there is hope...there is healing on the other side. His yoke is easy, we were not meant to carry these heavy burdens.

Are you ready to cast them aside? Are you packed and ready for this healing journey? There is joy, peace and love again!

Victory is born out of struggle. It is where we learn. We learn from our pain. Don't be afraid of it, face it, it's where you will grow.

Ruth, Naomi and Oprah experienced a unique bonding because of their experiences, like a support group. You can't learn from someone who hasn't walked in your shoes. People can't give you what they don't have. You forge great relationships from that bond.

Once you start to make sense of your pain, a support group can help you sort through it, with other women or men that have walked it.

When God begins to bless you remember who gave you the overabundance. Thank Him for the small and big things.

Life is for the living, get back into it. Give Him back the wheel, there is no better Driver!

I wasn't one to be transparent, it was and still is difficult for me. I held onto it with guilt and shame. I would open up just a little to close friends. But I never fully disclosed it all to anyone.

Some say nobody cares, keep it to yourself, everybody has a story and don't air your dirty laundry. My God said it is through your testimony others will be healed. You are a vessel in which I will work through. Back in 2016 when the Lord said it will be through your testimony others will see and know Jesus is the Healer, Provider a Mighty Counselor, I began this Healing Hearts Ministry.

It is not because I am special or that God cares more for me, it is however that I am a willing vessel for Him to mold me and shape me for His Glory.

1 John 5:9 - If we receive the testimony of men, the testimony of God is ... "If I alone testify about Myself, my testimony is not true. ... For we have heard it ourselves from His own mouth."

Psalms 119:26 "I will also speak of Your testimonies before kings and shall not be ashamed."

I am healed through the blood of Jesus. I will not be ashamed or offended by those who say nobody cares. Yes, He cares so much that He sends his vessels to work through to show you just how much He loves you and cares. He is for you!

When sabotage is in play in your life, whether you are self-destroying or you know someone is sabotaging you, it is destruction they seek.

Although there are many reasons to self-sabotage, this is really your subconscious trying to protect you, prevent pain and deal with deep-seated fear.

For this writing we are going to stay on the reasons we self-sabotage in our life or relationships. When we do this, we fear failure, or that we may look stupid or that we are hopelessness in a relationship working out.

We self-sabotage, we self-destruct, we ruin it out of fear, hurt or even self-hatred. Pain runs so deep; we might as well not even try!

How to stop this destructive behavior is to recognize it first. Call it what it is and identify your triggers. Learn to communicate and learn self-care.

It is a journey to find out about yourself and for many the pain is too much to bear. But the more you learn about yourself, the stronger you become. The more you learn to communicate you begin understanding.

The road to the cross is narrow, but the Hope of the world is there waiting for you with His arms wide-open.

Teach them while they are young and when they grow old, they will not depart far from the word. Proverbs 22:6

Or another translation; Teach children how they should live, and they will remember it all their life. Different meaning?

We are what we learn, we didn't pick or choose our parents but God knew you in your mother's womb. Some of us have had the gift of awesome parents, some of us not so much. Some have life so easy and some struggle every day to survive

God didn't promise us a rose garden, but He does say; keep His ways and He will stick closer to you than any friend.

Why is it life seems so easy for some, while others fight to eat? To this I know not the answer.

However, I do know I will never go hungry because He is my Provider. Put Him first in all things and He will make your paths straight. How do you put God first? Prayer the most powerful weapon in your arsenal!

How different my life would have been if I wasn't abused when I was young, didn't grow up poor and wasn't made fun of, no...it all made me into the woman I am today. God didn't waste a thing, He made me a warrior, strong, bold and my foundation built on Solid Rock.

When I wake up the enemy says, oh no she's awake because he knows who I serve. Thank you, my Jesus, without You I would not be where I am today. Praise Your Holy name.

Shame keeps us imprisoned to a past event. The definition of shame is a painful feeling of humiliation or distress caused by the consciousness of wrong or foolish behavior. Read that again, it's a feeling...that feeling can keep you tied to that event for years. No one else may even know, just you, your past and it torments you to this day.

Listen, there is no one without sin, except for 1 man who walked on this earth over 2000 years ago. We all have a past, we can either learn from it, garner wisdom from those who have moved on and learn how to let go.

I have the secret sauce, the miracle cure...want to know how? Keep reading...

Everyday all that I write in here daily is the journey of healing and letting go. Discover the tools, discover yourself and immerse yourself in the Word of God daily.

He is your secret sauce...Jesus is our Miracle. He took on our shame, so we can give it to Him and be free.

I carried shame around for years. It was so heavy like a chain and 100lb weight around my neck for 23 years. Imagine what that does to a person, keeping shame locked away inside you for 23 years! It torments you; it replays in your mind again and again. You can delete it!

Like a line drawn in the sand, I felt if I crossed over the shame, if I let it out, that it would break me. The complete opposite was true. It was the letting it out to someone safe, a woman of God that I was able to let go of that tormenting spirit of shame. That shame morphs into depression and suicidal thoughts.

It didn't break me like I thought, it freed me...oh praise the name of Jesus...I am free.

You too can be free of bondage. You have the choice to hold onto it or be free of it. This day what do you choose?

In Christianity, the word may have several meanings. Discernment can describe the process of determining God's desire in a situation or for one's life or identifying the true nature of a thing, such as discerning whether a thing is good, evil, or may even transcend the limiting notion of duality.

Apostle Paul mentions the gift of discerning of spirits in 1 Cor. 12:10. In the interpretation of this passage it says that these words mean the ability to tell who is spiritual and who is not, who is a prophet and who is not since at the time of Apostle Paul, there were many false prophets deceiving people.

Pray and ask the Lord to allow you to see the truth, to be able to see the false in the situation. Sometimes the enemy brings out wolves in sheep's clothing to get you off track.

Don't fall for the deception. Ask the Lord to open the eyes of your heart. Pray up, cover yourself and remember God is in control of all things. You have not because you ask not.

Dear Heavenly Father, you knew the number of hairs on our heads and You determine our days; you feed the sparrows of the air and you open doors no one can shut and shut doors no one can open. We trust you in our comings and our goings. We trust you Jesus. Amen

Roman's 13:1-7; Let every person be subject to the governing authorities. For there is no authority except from God, and those that exist have been instituted by God. Therefore, whoever resists the authorities resists what God has appointed, and those who resist will incur judgment. For rulers are not a terror to good conduct, but too bad. Would you have no fear of the one who is in authority? Then do what is good, and you will receive his approval, for he is God's servant for your good. But if you do wrong, be afraid, for he does not bear the sword in vain. For he is the servant of God, an avenger who carries out God's wrath on the wrongdoer. Therefore, one must be in subjection, not only to avoid God's wrath but also for the sake of conscience...

No matter which way this election turns out, we must pray that God is victorious.

I see posts that say you can't hate and be a Christian. This is an incredible misleading statement. Rather it should say you can't hate and be in a relationship with Jesus. We are human and prone to our emptions.

It is religion and old testament thinking putting God in a box.

I am a Christian, what does that mean to me? I have the Spirit of the Living Lord on the inside of me. His heart is my heart, it's a relationship with Him who sticks closer than a friend. He never leaves me or forsakes me.

I fall short of the Glory of God, my sin is as filthy rags, BUT He loves me through it and like a Loving Father, welcomes me back into His Arms every time I pray and ask forgiveness.

I am not religious; I am a child of God!

What choices will you make today? To make your bed, or not? To shower, to have a cup of coffee, or to exercise?

What about the choice to have joy, laughter or to be positive? Can you choose these things? Yes, of course, you have the power to choose positive over negative thoughts. You have the choice to plan out your day or just take it as it comes.

Joshua 24:15 choose for yourselves this day whom you will serve...

I choose the Lord and all His promises and blessings.

Think positive, speak positive and be positive; it causes a positive chain reaction!

"I am that I am". What does that mean? I believe it means different things to different people. To me, it was our Creator saying, He is to us what we need Him to be at a moment in time.

When we are sad, He is our Joy.

When we are out of sorts, He is our Peace.

When we are depressed, He is our Comforter.

When we are sick, He is our Healer.

When we are alone, He is closer than any friend.

When we don't know how we are going to eat, He is our Provider.

When we need medicine, He is our Doctor.

When we are in a legal battle, He is our Counselor.

The Great I Am, is what You need Him to be right now!

Jesus, great "I AM" and Lord of what is, said, "Come to me, all you who are weary and burdened, and I will give you rest." (Matthew 11:28).

Have you ever met someone and you instantly had a connection? Not just a love connection, but a friend? There's just something about them inside you that rises up inside you and bam, you really like this person and even today years later that connection still exists.

Now, the opposite being true, you meet someone and there is an instant feeling of not liking them, something inside you warns you to stay away. If you listened you probably saved yourself from an awful event. If you didn't listen, you have a story to tell.

Have you ever been walking, driving or going somewhere and something inside you warns you not to go inside or not to go?

We all need to listen to that voice! Get to know that voice, really well for it is that discerning Spirit, the Comforter, the Helper that Christ Jesus left here on earth until His work is done that resides on the inside of you.

God will wreck your plans when He sees that your plans are about to wreck you.

Holy Spirit come; I welcome You in this place. Walk with me, talk with me, I give this day over to You. Thank you, Lord Jesus.

Let go of unforgiveness today, it only makes you bitter.

Set yourself free by letting go!

Besides it doesn't hurt the other person, it hurts you in too many ways, stomach issues, anxiety, headaches and other illnesses.

Unforgiveness is like a cancer eating away at you from the inside. Feelings should be just visitors, let them come and let them go.

Say this...I forgive _____! You don't have to forget; you don't ever have to be a part of their life; but you do need to release it and get it out of you to allow healing into your body.

Do you only believe what you can see, touch or feel? Are you analytical, having to weigh and measure everything that is said?

Or are you a faith believer? Someone who believes without seeing, knowing God's word is true because God has proved to you through your faith that it will never return void?

Is it possible to read the Bible and still not believe? Is it possible to be "yea of little faith"?

Faith is a strong belief or trust in someone or something. A belief in the existence of God: strong feelings or beliefs. Therefore, if you are of little faith, it may be time for you to get big faith! How?

Exercise your faith. The Bible says Test me in this," says the LORD Almighty, "and see if I will not throw open the floodgates of heaven and pour out so much blessing that you will not have room enough for it. I will prevent pests from devouring your crops, and the vines in your fields will not cast their fruit," says the LORD Almighty. Malachi 3:10

God is not afraid of failing your test. Go ahead and let Him begin to show you just how Mighty He is. Everything you are going through is preparing you for what you have asked for.

When I was a baby, I talked like a baby, walked like a baby and now that I am all grown in Christ Jesus I walk like a warrior, I talk like He has already provided for me! Because I exercise my faith daily and my God shows up each and every time!

We sometimes want to fast forward into the future. I can't wait for this day to get over, or this week, or even this year.

But if we look, really look for the lesson's life is teaching us, perhaps we can slow down long enough to glean the lesson.

Everything and everyone leave a deposit in our journey if you will. Look at it and ask yourself what can I learn from this life lesson.

Remember grapes must be squashed to make wine, diamonds form under pressure, olives are pressed to release the oil and seeds grow in darkness. Whenever you feel crushed, under pressure or in darkness you are in a powerful place of transformation. Trust the process...

Keep learning, keep growing and keep moving. Don't get stuck! Trust in the Lord with all your heart.

Although we are in this world, the Bible says as CHRISTians (Christ followers), we are not of this world.

Jesus says we are to battle in the spirit, that our weapons are not carnal, that we war in the spirit. Everything that exalts itself against the knowledge of God, we are to bring those thoughts captive. Ephesians 6:11-17

We all have the Spirit of the Living God inside us, that we can call upon the Holy Spirit, that we war not against flesh and blood, but spirits within them.

Is this Sci-Fi, things to be afraid of? No, He did not give us a spirit of fear, but a Spirit of Authority to bring down strongholds.

If you don't know the Holy Spirit, get to know Him, for it is through Him we are able to cast out, put on and walk out God's Word.

2 Corinthians 10:5 Casting down imaginations, and every high thing that exalted itself against the knowledge of God, and bringing into captivity every thought to the obedience of Christ..

Listen to that small still voice, when you do you will wear the belt of Truth, the Breastplate of Righteousness, the Shield of Faith, the Helmet of Salvation...

At some point it has to go from being highlighted in your Bible to being written in your heart!

Ever had one of those days, weeks, months and even year! We all have had one of those years as 2020 goes into the history books. But for this topic, is weariness, burning the midnight oil or just plain burnt out from over-doing it.

And on the 7th day God rested. He told us to work for 6 days and then rest. But we don't, we fill our days and weeks with so many "have to's" that we forget ourselves. We cannot pour from an empty vessel.

Matthew 11:28-30 Come to me, all who labor and are heavy laden, and I will give you rest. Take my yoke upon you, and learn from me, for I am gentle and lowly in heart, and you will find rest for your souls. For my yoke is easy, and my burden is light."

Think about that for a moment, mediate on it and see what it means to you. We all over do it and wonder why our anxiety is through the roof. Doing it God's way brings about peace, healing and joy. Spend some time with the Lord, for He is Good! Prayer is the cure for a confused mind, a weary soul and a broken heart.

When sabotage is in play in your life, whether you are self-destroying or you know someone is sabotaging you, it is destruction they seek.

Although there are many reasons to self-sabotage, this is really your subconscious trying to protect you, prevent pain and deal with deep-seated fear.

For this writing we are going to stay on the reasons we self-sabotage in our life or relationships. When we do this, we fear failure, or that we may look stupid or that we are hopelessness in a relationship working out.

We self-sabotage, we self-destruct, we ruin it out of fear, hurt or even self-hatred. Pain runs so deep; we might as well not even try!

How to stop this destructive behavior is to recognize it first. Call it what it is and identify your triggers. Learn to communicate and learn self-care.

It is a journey to find out about yourself and for many the pain is too much to bear. But the more you learn about yourself, the stronger you become. The more you learn to communicate you begin understanding.

The road to the cross is narrow, but the Hope of the world is there waiting for you with His arms wide-open.

Teach them while they are young and when they grow old, they will not depart far from the word. Proverbs 22:6

Or another translation; Teach children how they should live, and they will remember it all their life. Different meaning?

We are what we learn, we didn't pick or choose our parents but God knew you in your mother's womb. Some of us have had the gift of awesome parents, some of us not so much. Some have life so easy and some struggle every day to survive.

God didn't promise us a rose garden, but He does say; keep His ways and He will stick closer to you than any friend.

Why is it life seems so easy for some, while others fight to eat? To this I know not the answer.

However, I do know I will never go hungry because He is my Provider. Put Him first in all things and He will make your paths straight. How do you put God first? Prayer the most powerful weapon in your arsenal!

How different my life would have been if I wasn't abused when I was young, didn't grow up poor and wasn't made fun of, no...it all made me into the woman I am today. God didn't waste a thing, He made me a warrior, strong, bold and my foundation built on Solid Rock.

When I wake up the enemy says, oh no she's awake because he knows who I serve. Thank you, my Jesus, without You I would not be where I am today. Praise Your Holy name.

I am proud of the woman I have become today because I went through a lot to become her.

Always asking yourself why or what leads you down a self-check path. It's not always the enemy or someone (thing) else. Sometimes it is us; we do it to ourselves.

Unresolved issues, thoughts or feelings can bring us back a year ago, 5 years ago or even more. Unresolved means simply something not finished/resolved.

It needs you to solve it. How do you do that? Ask yourself questions and like the root of a weed you don't want growing back again, you pluck it out by resolving it.

Ask yourself what triggered me; I felt excluded, I felt powerless, I felt judged or I felt blamed. Name it, then you can solve it.

Shame keeps us imprisoned to a past event. The definition of shame is a painful feeling of humiliation or distress caused by the consciousness of wrong or foolish behavior. Read that again, it's a feeling...that feeling can keep you tied to that event for years. No one else may even know, just you, your past and it torments you to this day. Feelings come and go, some we have to let go.

Listen, there is no one without sin, except for 1 man who walked on this earth over 2000 years ago. We all have a past, we can either learn from it, garner wisdom from those who have moved on and learn how to let go.

I have the secret sauce, the miracle cure...want to know how? Keep reading...

Everyday all that I write in here daily is the journey of healing and letting go. Discover the tools, discover yourself and immerse yourself in the Word of God daily.

He is your secret sauce...Jesus is our Miracle. He took on our shame, so we can give it to Him and be free.

I carried shame around for years. It was so heavy like a chain and 100lb weight around my neck for 23 years. Imagine what that does to a person, keeping shame locked away inside you for 23 years! It torments you; it replays in your mind again and again. The mind replays what the heart can't delete; you can delete it!

Like a line drawn in the sand, I felt if I crossed over the shame, if I let it out, that it would break me. The complete opposite was true. It was the letting it out to someone safe, a woman of God that I was able to let go of that tormenting spirit of shame. That shame morphs into depression and suicidal thoughts.

It didn't break me like I thought, it freed me...oh praise the name of Jesus...I am free.

You too can be free of bondage. You have the choice to hold onto it or be free of it. This day what do you choose?

Don't start your tomorrow with the broken pieces of yesterday. Tomorrow is a new day, begin it fresh.

Are you an enabler? A person or thing that makes something possible. A person who encourages or enables negative or self-destructive behavior in another.

We do it without even knowing or realizing the harm or codependency we create in the person or situation. We think we are helping or loving, but don't realize we are handicapping the person. We take away their decision-making by making it for them or just taking control and getting it done.

Step away for a moment and try to see it from another perspective. What handcuffs have you put on the person by taking control? What blindfold have you put over their ability to see? How has it cut them off at the knees because you keep stepping in?

Whether it is your children, spouse or a situation...step back, pause and ask yourself if I... _____will they?

Is it time to stop drinking milk and start eating solid food? The Lord wants us to grow up. Luke 2:40 And the child grew and became strong, filled with wisdom. And the favor of God was upon him.

Ask the Lord for wisdom, rest in His arms.

Roman's 13:1-7

Let every person be subject to the governing authorities. For there is no authority except from God, and those that exist have been instituted by God. Therefore, whoever resists the authorities resists what God has appointed, and those who resist will incur judgment. For rulers are not a terror to good conduct, but too bad. Would you have no fear of the one who is in authority? Then do what is good, and you will receive his approval, for he is God's servant for your good. But if you do wrong, be afraid, for he does not bear the sword in vain. For he is the servant of God, an avenger who carries out God's wrath on the wrongdoer. Therefore, one must be in subjection, not only to avoid God's wrath but also for the sake of conscience...

No matter which way this election turns out, we must pray that God is victorious.

I see posts that say you can't hate and be a Christian. This is an incredible misleading statement. Rather it should say you can't hate and be in a relationship with Jesus.

It is religion and old testament, put God in a box kind of thinking.

I am a Christian, what does that mean to me? I have the Spirit of the Living Lord on the inside of me. His heart is my heart, it's a relationship with Him who sticks closer than a friend. He never leaves me or forsakes me.

I fall short of the Glory of God, my sin is as filthy rags, BUT He loves me through it and like a Loving Father, welcomes me back into His Arms every time I pray and ask forgiveness. I fight my battles on my knees in worship.

If we have the choice to speak positive instead of negative, to choose joy and peace, then we have the choice to learn that our past is a learning experience and it only defines us...if and what we let it.

I am a failure, if you quit trying...learn from it and grow past it.

I have no money...are you a good steward over what you do have? What can you do to increase your income? Or decrease your bills? Choices!

We make daily decisions some out of habit, without realizing them. If we are intentional about our decisions and choices, we can make changes then for the better. Understanding ourselves is the 1st step.

Without change growth is impossible. Staying the same day in and day out; only you can make the decision to grow through it.

Open the eyes of my heart Lord, help me to make the right choices to leave the broken pieces and allow you to sew me back together again. Give me beauty for my ashes, joy for my sorrows and replace in me what needs to go in Jesus' name.

Someday you will see that you weren't falling apart, but falling into place.

With so much happening in just 6 months of 2020, your head might be spinning with what is right, who is right, we hear conspiracy theories, news, FB, people with their point of view...what do you do? Who do you believe?

Be careful what you see, listen to and what you allow in.

Propaganda is information, especially of a biased or misleading nature, used to promote or publicize a particular political cause or point of view.

Evil prevails when good people do nothing. What is evil? Wicked, bad, wrong, morally wrong, wrongful, immoral, sinful, ungodly, unholy, foul, vile, base, ignoble, dishonorable, corrupt, iniquitous, depraved, degenerate, villainous, nefarious, sinister, vicious, malicious, malevolent, demonic, devilish, diabolic, diabolical, fiendish, dark, black-hearted.

I can only say I choose to stand on the Word of God and what He says it right and true.

Isiah 5:20, What sorrow for those who say that evil is good and good is evil, that dark is light and light is dark, that bitter is sweet and sweet is bitter.

John 10:10, The thief comes only to steal and kill and destroy. I came that they may have life and have it abundantly.

God 1st! His Heart is His people. I choose to believe the Bible and not FB, news media or anything that is contrary to His word.

I choose to see you as God sees your heart. I may fall short, but God forgives me, will you?

What would Jesus do if He was walking here on earth today?

He would certainly preach about love and unity of His people. He would certainly go about healing and encourage us to do as He does.

What would Jesus do today? He would do as the Bible says, His word does not return void. He would go about doing our Father's business. Preaching, Healing, showing Grace, Mercy and Love.

Lord Jesus, come fall down on us. Heal us and our land. Bring unity and love to Your Children. Forgive us Jesus. We cry out to You. Turn your Eyes back on us. Restore Love and Healing to Your people. Thank you, Jesus! Jesus is the bridge between us and the Father.

Each morning we wake up, is a new chance to do something different.

There are 365 of them. Routines are great and needed, but if you are stuck in a rut and doing the same thing 365 days...it's time to change things up. What feels like the end is often the beginning!

God has given you a new morning, new beginnings, a chance for you to write a new chapter in your life. It is going to take YOU to make the changes. Why not start today?

The Bible is filled with God's promises to you, but they don't just come and knock on your door. It takes action on your part; it takes you getting up and out.

Need a job? Go and apply and then pray for God to open the door on the perfect job for you. Want a spouse, pray for God to prepare them and you for the day they are presented to you.

Philippians 4:6 "Do not worry about anything, but in everything, by prayer and petition, with thanksgiving, let your requests be made known to God."

God says, test me in this," says the LORD Almighty, "and see if I will not throw open the floodgates of heaven and pour out so much blessing that you will not have room enough for it. Malachi 3:10

Don't be like Naaman, he came to the prophet Elisha and got angry when he told him to bath in the muddy waters of the river. He turned away in rage...how dare he and turned around in rage. (2 Kings 5:11-12).

Sometimes our healing is a mud pie to the eye, or a dip in the muddy river. Sometimes our victory is to walk around a building 3 times with singing praise.

When our anger turns to rage, we stop listening, our thoughts become distorted to the truth. Naaman did eventually dip himself 7 times in the river and he was healed of his leprosy, but it wasn't that he listened to the prophet, it was a traveling buddy who talked sense into him.

He could have walked away not healed. What silly thing have you been asked to do and refused?

Things of the spirit sometimes doesn't make sense to our human mind, but the Holy Spirit knows.

Trust Him with all our heart and lean not to your own understanding and in all your way He will make them straight. Lord let your voice be the only voice I hear and trust.

Yeah, I'm sorry, I said I'm sorry. What do I have to be sorry for, I didn't do anything wrong? Or no acknowledgement at all to the offensive behavior.

When we don't acknowledge the behavior, we walk around hurting others, but mostly ourselves. Broken pieces lying all over, following us wherever we go; a trail of unforgiveness, pain and suffering.

If you don't want to apologize, check your reason why...still hurt? Angry? Or has it deeply embedded itself inside you and is now total bitterness?

If the hurt or anger is fresh and new; there is a process, a journey that needs to be taken to walk you through the hurt and pain.

If it has been years and has turned your stomach sour, it could be deeply embedded and your conscience has shifted the guilt to someone else; transferred the pain if you will. But you continue to be the one who suffers in silence.

Forgiveness is a wonderful gift to you. It brings about peace in letting go. Let today be the 1st step in the process of forgiveness. Start with...it may take me a while but forgive me. I've held onto this long enough...I want to let go and forgive.

God says you weren't rejected, He hid your worth and value because they were not assigned to your destiny.

Are you a control person? A place for everything and everything in its place? The definition of control is the power to influence or direct people's behavior or the course of events.

Do you try to influence or direct people's behavior or course of events?

The key to this definition is "power to", when we realize God is the One in Control and that He is where our Power lies; we give ourselves up and over to Him. Because we are not in control to change a person or the course of events.

Our prayers touching the ears of our Heavenly Father through Christ Jesus. Now, this is where we watch the course of events change.

This is where we watch Him change the hearts of our husbands, children and even those that wish evil upon us.

The sooner we realize we can only control our reaction and the words that we speak, the quicker we will reap peace. Be anxious for nothing, but pray about everything and for everyone.

Let go today, give this day to Him, lay it at His capable feet and watch things change. Because only God is in control. Even God can't change free will; but He works on the inside changing hearts.

No matter what we feel, think or know; we are not here on earth to just live our life and die. We are not here for ourselves.

(Matthew 18:12–14) and (Luke 15:3–7). It is about a shepherd who leaves his flock of ninety-nine sheep in order to find the one which is lost.

We, yes, you and I are the hands, feet, eyes, ears and heart of the Great Shepard. If our purpose is to save the 1, for Jesus that is enough. Remember the above parable.

If you are 20, 30, 40, 50, 60's...no matter what age, God is not done with you. You were born and selected to fulfill your destiny.

Each trial you go through is a life lesson learned so you can have the empathy and experience to help someone else going through what you have learned. You are His earthen angel.

Look at all the strength that you have from every experience that you have lived through. Those are life lessons for you to help the hurt and broken hearted.

People always ask, what is my destiny...be an angel and go help someone today.

God uses broken people like you and me to rescue His broken people.

Trust in the Lord with all your heart...we need to because He knows what is best for us. We are emotional beings and those emotions get in the way of clear sound thinking. But Your will be done!

We sometimes think we know better, we want to control the outcome, but we aren't in control. Get used to praying, but Your will be done Lord. His ways are not ours... (here comes that word again), but His ways are the best for us.

He is history, He is omnipresent and He is the future. Who better to trust than your Heavenly Father! God not only sees where you are but He sees where you are to be.

There is no expiration date on how long a person should grieve. It is a personal experience, one that is different person to person. Some people with good intentions may tell you it's time to move on but you are still grieving. The hurt and pain is still too real.

Grief can be a divorce, a loss of a person, which can be living or through death. The pain and hurt is the same, it's deep and penetrates all aspects of your life and mind. You go to sleep with it and awake with it and it looms over you day in and day out. I have grieved the loss of many loved ones, a divorce and a 4-year separation as well as empty-nest syndrome and the grief is real. Well intended people will try to make you feel better.

When you are ready, find someone to talk to, or a group that you can share your grief with. The healing process is when you go deep into your emotions and come out the other side at peace.

The thing is don't get stuck in your grief, keep learning and growing from the loss of that relationship and move forward. Remember there is no expiration date to how long you grieve. Don't stay there for too long.

He heals the broken hearted and binds up their wounds Psalms 147:3

Your words are powerful containers. A man is as he thinks. What are the tapes in your mind saying about you?

Break the negative ranting of your mind. Visualization and speaking positive out loud can help break the negative messages you send yourself.

Start today with; I am a good person, I am loveable, I have awesome skills, God calls me the Apple of His Eye. Go ahead try it...I am _____ fill in the blank.

Make your list of your positive attributes, visualization and mantras that you will begin saying about your life. Watch your life change!

A negative mind will never give you a positive life.

Faith is...knowing God's word is true.

Faith is...His word shall go forth.

Faith is...if only I can touch the hem of His garment, I will be healed.

Faith is...when I pray He hears.

Faith is...if I ask in Jesus name, it shall be done.

Faith is...that the Heavenly Father knows my name.

Faith is...when I say to that mountain...it shall be moved.

Faith is...believing not seeing

Faith is...He inhabits the praises of His people.

Faith is...the Holy Spirit resides in me because of what Jesus has done on the Cross.

Faith is...greater are the things you shall do in Jesus name.

Faith is...God said it...enough said!

You are God's Masterpiece!

Did you know there are levels of trust? I trust them as far as I can throw them, I'll believe it when I see it or I trust until...

But God wants us to trust, believe and have faith even when we don't hear Him, see Him or feel Him...that is BIG faith and trust!

All Scripture is breathed out by God and profitable for teaching, for reproof, for correction, and for training in ...

He tells us to ask in Jesus's name, lay our petitions before Him and the believe it is ours. Declare it! Believe it! Expect it! Be purposeful in your prayers.

He's waiting for you to talk to Him. He is faithful, He is just and He promises in His word. Oh, hallelujah our Father is good!

Water, without it we can't live, life as we know it wouldn't exist and too much of it...well you know flood waters are not clean. They are filled with debris and until the flood waters recede, stay out of the water!

Once they do recede, that's when the real work begins...the cleanup.

When we shower or soak in a tub the effects of water are cleansing. When we go to the beach or sit by a running creek, the sounds of the waves and running water has a calming effect on us humans. A day at the beach is calming, a day hiking to a waterfall is breathtaking...is it any wonder why Jesus used water baptism to put down the old flesh and come up out of the water a new creature in Christ?

We are laid down in a watery grave, our old dirty debris ridden self is left in the water and we arise refreshed, cleaned and oh so beautiful!

Have you been baptized? Our Savior walks on water!

Pain is a physical hurt from a surgery or accident. Agony is a mental suffering. You know the kind, its unrelenting, it won't let you go and the pain is unbearable.

Anguish is severe mental or physical pain. Being extremely worried about something. Suffering the state of undergoing pain, distress, or hardship.

What do all of these have in common? Pain, suffering, agony and anguish?

Sometimes we can't escape it like from surgery, but it passes. Other times we hold onto it like a familiar coat. We get stuck in the comfort of the suffering. What?!

Have you ever seen or not heard from someone for years and you find them right where you left then 5, 10, 15 even 20 years ago; still in agony, suffering needless anguish because they are stuck in their muck and mire.

Listen, pain is there to make us feel, to use it to grow, become stronger, and work through it just like in physical therapy. You don't have to stay stuck. You are choosing the comfort of where you are verses making the changes, going through the hard work to get yourself out of the pain.

It's a long difficult journey going deep inside yourself. Taking the holy ghost flashlight through the crevices of your heart and past. No one likes to look at themselves, can it be me?

We didn't get here all by ourselves, we made choices along life's way. Those choices are yours. Haven't you wasted enough of your life in agony, pain, suffering and being stuck?

Today, make the choice to do the hard (very hard) work of growing and changing. It all starts with admitting that you are stuck, that you need to change and grow. Help is out there, but you have to want it more than staying the same.

I threw in the towel and God threw it back and said, wipe your face you are almost there.

Jesus held the highest position in heaven, but He came to us with the heart of a servant. That word servant has a bad connotation in our world today. A servant was free, was not a slave, in the Bible having the heart of a servant meant to be humble and be right with God.

Listen, it is not all about you, it is all about Him. We were not put on this earth to please ourselves. When we humble ourselves, get pride out of the way and help someone; the feeling is priceless. The more you recognize who you are in relationship to Him, the more you embrace humility.

Being a servant of God it takes listening, empathy, healing, awareness, persuasion, conceptualization, foresight, stewardship, commitment to the growth of people, and building community.

It is one of the most difficult and time-consuming work, but also the most gratifying.

When you see a volunteer giving of their time for the work of the Kingdom, thank them, because their heart is pure, humbled and right with the Lord to help as many people during their time on earth.

If your desire is to serve the Lord with all your heart, you are not alone – God is with you. It is all about Him, His people and His Kingdom.

I was asked how to pray. There is no magic answer, it is really just you talking to God, it is that simple. Like anything the more, you pray you develop a stronger prayer.

Prayer does not have to be complicated, it is your way of talking to God.

I always begin with thanking Him 1st, giving Him all the Glory. I then ask for His Will to be done no matter what I am asking, because if it is not of God, I do not want it.

Then I ask Him for what I need, (laying your petitions before Him). I ask Him to forgive me and then pray for family, friends, my ministry, the ladies in my group and our nation and leaders.

I always pray back His word to remind Him and mostly me that His word DOES NOT RETURN VOID!

Every time I pray, I believe I have what He says; expectations, because I know He hears me. Unstoppable God that is who I serve!

I am a mess today, I am hopeless, I am unlovable...instead say this, I may have messed up today but I have a mess-cleaner that forgives me. I serve the Hope of this world. He loves me so much that He sent His only son to die for me.

We can change our thoughts and words. Anything life throws at you can be changed, look for it, say it out loud, there is POWER in our words.

We were bought up to be one way by parents that may not have known how to teach. But that doesn't mean I am all those things spoken over me for years.

I broke those ties in Jesus's name. I am a Child of the Living God. I am what He says I am! After all, He is my Authority, what He says is the final word, not man.

Name those things and cast them out forever more in Jesus's name. Fill them with His words. Once we name it, that thing loses power over us.

Marriage is hard work, but as you talk through the rough patches and sometimes just agree to disagree. When faith collides with reality, it flexes and holds on until victory emerges. Love prevails.

Relationships don't last because of the good times, they last because how the couple handled the bad times; with patience, kindness and love.

If your eyes are good, your whole body will be full of light. ... If then the light within you is darkness, how great is that darkness! (Mt 6:22–23)1.

How deep is your darkness? I don't have any darkness in me! Oh really, Jesus alludes to ancient conventions of the eye and light in his teaching on treasures, undivided loyalties and anxiety with regard to the necessities of life. What are your eyes focused on? Is it all for you? Or do you look for ways to shine your light? Looking for ways to help others?

Let your light shine so bight before men, that the darkness cannot creep in. Darkness brings fear and anxiety. The light expels the darkness, fear and anxiety.

Let the Light of this world in. Let Him shine brightly within you. Find something to praise God for, change complaining into blessings. Give Him all the Glory.

Name your Blessings…

#IVoted2020 no matter who wins tomorrow the Lord God Reigns.

Whether you like them or not, the Lord God Reigns.

Whatever, whomever tomorrow put your trust in the Lord God Almighty that He already knew the outcome.

Peace, I say unto you, His Peace that surpasses all understanding.

Whichever way this goes, the people have voted and may His Glory shine upon America.

I am putting my trust in Jesus, may the Holy Spirit move Mightily upon this land.

Never before has it been so easy to give your opinion, argue and fight. The day of computers, social media platforms and being confined at home; being told where you can go or can't go. People sitting at home behind their smartphone, iPad or laptops typing words...so many words.

Are they thinking before they write? Or are they writing with no care where their words will end up. Who will read them? What kind of head space is the reader of your words in? Will they encourage the reader, or will they tear down? Do you even care?

Your writings are powerful containers of words, having the power to tear down or edify someone. The reader of your words could be contemplating suicide and your post just pushed them over the edge. Someone's child, sibling or parents. Someone was at home reading your words and it made them break their sobriety.

I can't be responsible for any of that! Really, the Bible says our words have the power of life or death...this day choose to encourage. Proverbs 18:21

We see and hear enough disappointment in life. Every one of us with past and present problems, hurts and pain. You can either choose to be a part of the problem, or choose life, edification and to help write about the beauty in the world.

We all see and hear enough darkness, it is all around us today the devil isn't hiding; he's out in plain sight.

I for one grow weary of this world! But praise God, I may live in this world; but my ways are His ways, my thoughts line up to His words and I choose today to speak boldly and tell you the Hope of the world is named Jesus and He is waiting to do battle on your behalf.

In my group sessions I teach about tools to use when encountering past hurts or present-day situations.

We go over each one during our 7-month course, to equip them with practical resources to be able to cope through this journey of healing. Healing is a long process, having to approach each hurt and relearn how to deal with them.

No drugs, no drinking and no numbing devices. It is all the Lord Jesus and the women's willingness to embrace this journey. Their healing is as much as they soak in the messages given in group sessions and reading the books assigned to them.

Courageously sharing and taking about what they have learned and applying it to their lives.

This is the short list of Tools in your Toolbelt:

1. Pause - don't react
2. Take 3 deep cleansing breathes, in through your nose and out through your mouth.
3. Setting healthy boundaries.
4. Not everything requires an answer.
5. MOST IMPORTANTLY GO VERTICAL IN ALL SITUATIONS
6. Learn to let the small stuff go.
7. Learn to forgive others and most importantly yourself.
8. Learn more about yourself, becoming self-aware.
9. Learning your triggers, buttons, your red flags.
10. In all situations as yourself; how, what, where, when and why?
11. Listen to understand not to respond. Hear what the person is saying. Don't listen to respond.
12. Ask clarifying questions, don't assume.
13. Be in balance; mentality, spiritually, physically and emotionally.
14. Make lists to stay organized.

15. When communicating always strive for win/win resolutions rather than a lose/lose or a win/lose.
16. Change your perspective.
17. Listen to praise and worship music, go into the presence of God.

The enemy is out in plain sight and you don't even see him. He walks among you and you don't see him. He fills your vision with images and you decern they are good. He presents lies to you and you think they are good, pictures on tv and you are riled up yes, yes, they must be true.

Anything, any word, thought or action contrary to God's word is not good. We are to line our thoughts, words and actions up with His words. Not the media, news or say so. Your authority is through Christ Jesus.

Isaiah 5:20 Woe to those who call evil good and good evil. You say wrong is right, darkness is light, and bitter is sweet. You are doomed! You call evil good and call good evil.

A tree bearing fruit is good. That means the person you are idolizing, ask yourself are they bearing good fruit or dead rotten ones? Taking God's words and conforming to what you see, think or feel = truth.

Idolizing color or anything before the Lord (news, social media or your phones), what does the Bible say: You shall have no other gods before me. This is expressed in the Bible in Exodus 20:3, Matthew 4:10, Luke 4:8 and elsewhere, e.g.: Ye shall make you no idols nor graven image, neither rear you up a standing image, neither shall ye set up any image of stone in your land, to bow down unto it: for I am the Lord your God.

Jeremiah 17:5 Thus says the Lord: "Cursed is the man who trusts in man and makes flesh his strength, whose heart turns away from the Lord.

Where is your trust today? Where is your faith today? It had better be with the Creator and not the created. For Only He is Good. His word is truth, it has to come to pass, because it does not return void.

Open your eye, see through the veil of lies and deceit. Look around you, is it lining up with God's word? Is it producing fruit.

Lies, burning cities, looting, killing, murder, abortions up to full term, beating people, no free will, government thinking and doing for you, displaying only the news and images that they want you to see, is this fair? We are not the judge only God can judge because He is Good, just and Right.

People get ready, you have idolized many images before God and He is not pleased.

Lord God, I stand in the gap for America asking you Lord my God, to turn your face back upon us. Don't leave your many children that love and listen to you. Forgive them Father, forgive the news media, social media and the people that have turned it from news to propaganda to turn the minds of the people.

Bless them Lord for they are blinded. We call out to Jesus, come let Your Holy Spirit pour out on the earth, let Him reign Jesus. Come Holy Spirit move about this earth.

It's a dangerous thing, to get a hard heart.

After years of mistreatment, being misunderstood and being taken advantage of, being callous is easy.

Forgive, you don't have to forget, but let go so that you can move forward with a loving, caring and sensitive heart.

A hard heart will lead you into years of disappointment. Hurt people, hurt others.

A sensitive heart opens you up to years of love.

It take more energy to hate than to love.

It all starts here with the truth. Why are there so many versions of the truth? Like the old game telephone, we used to play in a circle, one would whisper in each other's ear what they heard person #1 say. By the time it got to the last person in the circle, it wasn't even close to what was originally stated. Our ears can deceive us.

Reality vs perception. We have our eyes that see, but our eyes can fail us in the situation too. If we are shown imagines all day long eventually you succumb to the images; they become your reality. Our eyes can be deceiving.

Then, there's our ears, we become what we listen to. What do you choose to allow to enter your spirit? Words are powerful, choose wisely what you listen to.

We also receive in our minds, we read something and our mind is already at work interpreting what you are reading.

So, what is the truth? What you hear, read or see? If we can be easily moved, how do we know the truth Discerning requires you to research the truth. It is using the wisdom given to us, to seek the truth to those things that are hidden.

Cor. 12:10. In the interpretation of this passage it says that these words mean the ability to tell who is spiritual and who is not, who is prophet and who is not since at the time of Apostle Paul, there were false prophets deluding people.

I pray that you use your ears to hear the truth, your eyes to read the truth, your mind to meditate on His word and your heart to discern the spiritual truth and false prophets in today's world.

Remember the truth shall set you free! You will never find yourself unless you face the truth of your past.

It takes a lot of energy to hate and to be angry. It is exhausting to be in pain.

Have you ever had an operation and been in pain? You are so exhausted; it strips you of all energy. Taking a shower, you are exhausted by doing the everyday things for yourself.

Anger hurts, it makes everything inside you bitter. Your face shows the world what your insides feel like.

Bitterness turns into acid reflux; peptic ulcers form from the acid in your stomach and you walk around carrying this bitterness. The door to the enemy has opened, he has you hook line and sinker.

Bitterness is the door for him to come and make a whole lot of changes within you. Soon you are addicted to social media, watching news all day long or listening to wrong music feeding the anger, pain and bitterness.

You can change it right now. STOP watching, stop listening and get that anger, bitterness and hatred out of you in Jesus's name.

You have free will, it is your choice to stop watching, it is your choice to end your family feuding but agreeing to disagree. You are only in control of you.

Set up healthy boundaries when with friends or family choose not to talk about issues that divide you.

It is so much easier to smile, love and look at yourself rather than others. Lord change me, for it all starts with you!

Father, I ask for forgiveness, Lord Jesus, take the wheel today, drive my path toward Righteousness and turn my path away from all evil. Holy Spirit forgive me for grieving you. I delight myself in You. Lord, change me, show me where I went wrong and help me to stay on the path of Righteousness for Your name's sake. I bind and rebuke any evil thing that has come up against me, anything that I have allowed in I close the door by the authority given to me, in Jesus's name. Amen

Ever notice how we judge or criticize others or even ourselves. Watch carefully what comes out of your mouth, our words are containers of power. Ever notice what you judge or criticize is what you don't like within yourself?

Matthew 7:5...pull the plank out of your own eye.

We need to be more concerned about that speck in us and work in making ourselves the best that we can be so that when we run into that person we want to judge, we can change our response and reaction to one of love and perhaps being a vessel that God put that person there for you to minister to.

Our criticizing does damage to us as well, we find fault with, censure, denounce, condemn, attack, lambaste, disapprove of, cast aspersions on, pour scorn on, disparage, deprecate, malign, vilify, and run down. These words are powerful and not of love.

Next time you want to criticize someone or even yourself think of the words above. Do you really want to give power to disparage or condemn others or yourself with the power of your words?

We become what we judge and criticize. Change your mindset, change your world.

When someone walks out of your life let them go. When we fight so hard to keep them, we push them further away. Remember everyone that comes in our lives is for a season, a reason and we learn from them. They deposit either good or bad. We have to be mindful of who we hang with.

Victory is born out of struggle.

Ruth 1:14 "Oprah kissed her mother-in-law goodbye." Her part in Oprah's life was over, she departed.

We need to acknowledge when something is over, otherwise we will struggle to keep it. If God meant for it to be, it will! Their leaving is no surprise to God...He's got something better for you.

Get showered, get dressed, eat, and move on. Those who belong in your life will remain. We need to trust and focus on the One who always has our back. I trust You Jesus!

Do you find a man sexy or good looking when you see past his outer shell? Our marriage has been a Rollercoaster of ups and downs.

Cinderella is a fairy tale! You have to kiss a lot of frogs to find your prince charming. But even then, your prince may turn back into a frog some days.

Marriage is hard work, day in and day out taking the good and bad. The secret to the ones that have been married for a long time? They never gave up on each other, there was no back door. The D-word never enters their lips.

They are committed to stay, talk it out and make their marriage work. But what about love? Listen, through my almost 20 years of marriage, there were days I barely liked him, but my love in my heart never ceased.

Love matures, it changes over the years, we are in it to win it... staying together, we are stronger.

No matter what, I love my husband, he is a good man, who loves the Lord and his wife. We struggle, we fuss and sometimes fight (but even our fights have matured). Does day to day get mundane? It's up to both of you to change it up.

We are united, one and God is always the head of our household. We admit to each other our faults and we forgive...

When anxiety rises, or when fear tries to come upon you, what is it that you do?

Think about that for a moment, do you run to social media? Dr. Google? Or do you go vertical giving it all to the only One that can change things?

It is what we do in the midst of the storm that matters. Can you quietly sleep in the boat that is being tossed to and fro?

Real peace is what we do while we are in the midst of chaos. Choose the Peace that surpasses all understanding! My Jesus, My Peace.

As God fearing children, we think He is to be feared, but He is to be respected and that we are to know Him intimately. When we know Him intimately, then we respect Him as the One and Only Living God.

When I was young, I feared the wrath of God, then I learned of His Love, Grace and Mercy. I learned it is our enemies that need to fear His wrath; vengeance is mine says the Lord.

I learned about His Peace and how to rest in His word. I learned when I feel like quitting, He is there right alongside me.

I learned when I am lonely, I am never alone. When I am upset, He is always there with an answer. I learned of His unfailing Love for His children.

I learned that He is my Provider and when I quit trying so hard in the flesh and lay it at the feet of Jesus...He always provides!

I learned He has a destiny for each of us and that He is waiting for you.

Today, most people are living life from the outside in. Whatever is happening externally affects you.

God calls us to live in the spirit, that we live life from the inside out, so whatever is happening externally we live by faith, not by sight.

We are not to be affected by what we see, instead we believe in those things not seen. "So, we fix our eyes not on what is seen, but on what is unseen, since what is seen is temporary, but what is unseen is eternal." 2 Corinthians 4:18

Are you easily moved by sight? Or do you rely on your trust and belief in God? As society moves to take away our beliefs, we are to stand and rise up even stronger in Christ Jesus.

In all circumstances take up the shield of faith, with which you can extinguish all the flaming darts of the evil one...Ephesians 6:16

Be watchful, stand firm in the faith, act like men, be strong. 1 Corinthians 16:13

These are the days we need to be David's, while the world falls apart, we stand in Truth and His Light!

Be a Lion, be a David...James 4:7 Submit yourselves therefore to God. Resist the devil, and he will flee from you.

Taking someone or something for granted. You know Givers will give and Takers will take, but we teach people how to treat us. It always begins and ends with you.

If you start out a relationship (any relationship, work, family or friends) and you are the Giver; you have taught them no matter what, no matter the treatment...you give.

The Giver eventually feels taken for granted, disgruntled and left with the feeling of why; I've done so much for them...we teach people how to treat us.

Now the opposite is not true here, the Taker doesn't feel remorse, you are giving and they are taking. But the bank account for you, (emotional bank account) becomes depleted and you need to be filled up (appreciated).

Learning about you and why you do the things you do, is a good place to start. Givers can no more turn into a taker, than a taker turn into a giver...it's who you are. But this is a big but, you can learn to have boundaries, self-respect and value; knowing when to start and stop filling up your emotional bank account. You can't serve from an empty vessel.

Can you gain respect from a taker or a relationship that is already established? Yes, this will take longer as you set healthy boundaries, eventually they will learn to respect them.

Definition of respect a feeling of deep admiration for someone or something elicited by their abilities, qualities, or achievements. Respect, also called esteem, is a positive feeling or action shown towards someone or something considered important, or held in high esteem or regard.

Do you value yourself? Do you find yourself valued? The Lord does, so begin today letting your light shine and show you are valued and esteemed by your Father in heaven. He thought so much of you that He sent His Only Son to die for you.

Have you ever had a persistent feeling of ill will or resentment resulting from a past insult or injury?

Have you ever grumbled or murmured at any person or thing, or entertained, or had an envious or covetous feeling, and did or gave anything unwillingly?

The above means you held a grudge against someone. To hold a grudge is to set ourselves up as judge and jury—to determine that one person's wrong, should not be forgiven. The Bible say only God judges, but as humans we all do, judge, criticize and hold grudges.

We sometimes hold a feeling and we don't even know why, we can't put a name to the feeling.

Leviticus 19:18 Thou shalt not .... bear any grudge against the children of the people.

We feel things in layers, the 1st is never the real reason it is usually the byproduct of the root cause. Your job is you, not anyone else and to find the root cause. Therein lies the answer.

A grudge leads to bitterness, envy, judging, cynical, hurt, hate, anger and complaining. Complaining blocks your blessing. Bitterness is resentful cynicism that results in an intense antagonism or hostility toward others.

Satan has you hook, line and sinker!

The above is all the "feelings" and emotions that you need to be in control of. It doesn't mean you will never feel them, we are human.

It does mean we are to bring every thought captive. Process it and come to your resolution and then respond, don't react and don't assume you know. Don't block your blessings by grumbling.

Leave it at the Cross, let it go and be at peace. "get rid of all bitterness, rage and anger, brawling and slander, along with every form of malice." It then goes on to tell us how to deal with such bitterness and its fruits by being "kind and compassionate to one another, forgiving each other, just as in Christ God forgave you" (Ephesians 4:31-32).

We all are in search of answers, knowledge and the reason of life. Knowledge we garner through information or experience but wisdom in the Bible is the word of knowledge it is a spiritual gift listed in 1 Corinthians 12:8. It has been associated with the ability to teach the faith, but also with forms of revelation similar to prophecy. It is closely related to another spiritual gift, the word of wisdom.

The word of Wisdom comes from above. Webster's dictionary defines knowledge as "the fact or condition of being aware of something." It also defines wisdom as "ability to discern inner qualities and relationships." In Scripture we are told that "The fear (reverence) of the Lord is the beginning of wisdom, and the knowledge of the Holy One is insight." Proverbs 9:10

To seek Wisdom is to find what the Lord gives so freely.

The seven gifts of the Holy Spirit are wisdom, understanding, counsel, fortitude, knowledge, piety, and fear of the Lord.

Get Wisdom today, seek and you will find, knock and He will answer...He is waiting for you to interact (relationship) with you.

Ever notice how much people complain today? It's too hot outside or it's snowing outside, the list goes on...complaining stops the blessing. It instills in you a spirit of negativity. Nothing measures up. You become your words.

Try for 24 little hours to not allow 1 word of negativity to exit your lips. It won't be easy! Each thought of a negative situation, turn it around to positive and see how your attitude shifts.

Especially when it comes to us, we are our worst judge and critic. We need to train our minds to hold every thought captive BEFORE it exits our mouth. 2 Corinthians 10:5

We need to guard our mouths; thoughts and it will show through our lifestyles. "From the fruit of their mouths..." we either reap a harvest of good fruit or bad fruit. You choose today.

Lord, set a guard over my mouth; keep watch over the door of my lips. Psalms 141:3

We have all but lost the language of physical touch in our world today. As humans we need it, we thrive on it and God made us to interact through physical touch.

Why is our society so disconnected? Why do we have so many with mental illness today? Society tells us to be more to get more, to buy this or that to make an impression.

Our lives are so enthralled in our phones that no one looks up any more. We are desensitized by games, texting and emails that face to face or even phone calls (to hear the voice of a friend or family member) is becoming the norm. It separates us even more.

God calls us to fellowship; His word says do not forsake the assembly of His people. Why? Proverbs 18:1 says a man who isolates himself, rages against the truth.

Ever feel cabin fever after being stuck in the house for 24 hours, 48 hours, even 72 hours? Isolation is not good for man, that is why God made Eve. He saw it was not good for man to be alone.

So, what is it that is stopping you today from reaching out? Fear? Pride? Don't like people or gatherings? Make the change, be the change...step outside and stop looking horizontal-start looking up for we serve an awesome God.

Besides it's not about us, it's all about Him.

This year, was a year of valleys and mountaintop experiences.

At this phase of my life, I count each one a blessing. One is a learning experience and the other a teaching tool.

I've learned to shift my paradigm and bring my thoughts into conformity with what I know to be truth (God's word).

I set short-term goals because at this stage, I don't know how many days I have left and it's best to live in the present. So, each morning I rise, is another day to be a blessing to others, encourage others, and thank God for another day to experience life.

I look forward to the upcoming year for God fulfilling my destiny, to continue to serve the ladies in my group and watch their awesome transformation into strong women of God.

May you find the upcoming year, to be a year of blessings, no matter what valleys you may experience. May you find encouragement and understanding.

Thank you, my Lord, for using me as your servant here on earth. Be a blessing in_____.

Houses are still decorated with Christmas. The New Year on the horizon and expectations are at an all-time low. Why not, with the year we all had, 2020 will not be missed but will go down in history.

But, did you know the Great I Am is History? He is the Future, the Beginning and the End. He knows, He is Victory.

But, is your faith up there with His Capabilities? Or do you waiver and lose trust? No matter, what my eyes see and my ears hear...I trust you Jesus. No matter! I trust You Lord.

Going into the New Year, leave the broken pieces of your past and begin 2021 anew, fresh and with complete faith in the Only Trustworthy One! Trust in His Strength to get you through.

Matthew 9:21 For she said within herself, If I may but touch his garment, I shall be whole.

It's a choice, a decision you make...isn't it time to be made whole?

As the New Year approaches and we close out the old and ready ourselves for the new, we can't help but bring our old self with us, into the New Year.

God gives us new mornings each day. We are able to do something different each day, but we are creatures of habit and continue to do the same thing, each day and each year...nothing changes.

Challenge yourself, not just this year, but each morning to not only do something different...be and think differently.

How? Make subtle changes in the way you do daily things. Keep the healthy habits, but break the bad ones.

Stay balanced, if your wheel of physical, emotional, spiritual and mental is out of whack, get back into balance.

Make a list, name the changes you want to make:

Persevere
Deeper Faith
Courage
Exercise
Eating healthy
Boundaries...add yours here.

Stay focused and don't bring the broken pieces of yesterday into your future.

Isaiah 43:19 "See, I am doing a new thing!

What will your new thing be? Name it, do it, be it...without change, growth is impossible.

New Year's Eve will be different around the world tonight. No gatherings, no NYC to watch the ball drop, restaurants closed and people socially distancing at home...some alone.

Proverbs 18:1 – A man who isolates himself seeks his own desires; he rages against all wise judgment.

Genesis 2:18, Then the Lord God said, "It is not good that the man should be alone...

Be fearless. You are never alone." - Joshua 1:9. 1 Corinthians 2:5-9, "...so that your faith might not rest in the wisdom of men but in the power of God...it is not wisdom of this age or of the rulers of this age, who are doomed to pass away. But we impart a secret and hidden wisdom of God."

Don't rely on man, the government or even some friends. Look up to the Holy One to give you His Peace, His Wisdom and His Grace, Love and Mercy.

Anything less, we are not relying on the Chain-breaker, Way-maker, the One and Only who determines the outcome.

It's your prayers, time spent with Him and laying your petitions before Him that changes to course of history.

Go in your war room and begin fighting against wickedness, evil...For our struggle is not against flesh and blood, but against the rulers, against the authorities, against the powers of this dark world and against the spiritual forces of evil in the heavenly realms. Ephesians 6:12

Have you ever had a friend placed on your heart? Someone you haven't seen or spoken with in a while? That feeling of relentless urging?

I know that feeling as the Holy Spirit placing someone on my heart to reach out and pray. The first day I whispered under my breathe for her. The second day, I even told my husband, I need to call her. Today, His urging was do it, call her and that I did.

Listen, we all have things going on in our lives. No one escapes pain, hurt, sickness, financial issues and the list goes on. But what can make a difference is PRAYER!

Don't put on a smiley mask to the world. We were not made to carry such burdens. Reach out to a praying woman or man of God and let them pray for you.

Lay your petitions before Him, His yoke is easy...all it takes is prayer.

If you are going through something and you need prayer, please message me.

How can I pray for you today?

Truth is sometimes hard to swallow. Truth hurts, many don't see the truth or even want to know the truth. What is the truth?

It is different than fact and is sometimes blurred right in front of us. It's the absolute truth, the ultimate truth, I swear to it.

What is truth? Does it have different meanings and does it change?

A fact, is something that's indisputable, based on research and quantifiable measures. Facts go beyond theories. They're proven through calculation and experience, or they're something that definitively occurred in the past. Truth is entirely different; it may include fact, but it can also include belief.

Therefore, truth can change based on belief. My truth may not be your truth, then based on my belief. But facts are undeniable. They are investigated, researched and beyond theory.

The root word of truth is ver, the English vocabulary word, includes verdict. The truth can be found trough research and includes the verdict. But are verdicts, always, right? The root ver is easily recalled through the word very, for when something is very good, it's "truly" good.

Jesus said He is the Truth, the Way and the Life...John 14:6, you see Jesus is Good!

We can change and manipulate words and truth can change but Jesus remains the same. He is always Good.

No matter what you see (our eyes can deceive us), no matter what you hear (our ears can deceive us), God is good all the time and that fact has been weighed, measured and verified in my heart forever.

As you can see there are many truths but My God will never fail. His Word never returns void. He is Good all the time.

Doubt can be cast over or on something or someone. It can happen with just speaking certain words that can be throwed forcefully (casting).

Our words are powerful, loose lips sink ships, or have the power to destroy a life, that someone took a life-time to build. Our words cast a shadow over that person and it can damage them for years or for that matter their lifetime.

Today, so many words are spoken by us, in jest, to destroy, to gossip, to give your opinion (we all have them) and want to respond.

An average man speaks 7,000 words in the course of a day, an average woman speaks 20,000 words in one day, some speak much more than that. Of your 7,000 -20,000 words you will use today; how many of them will be used to help, uplift and be kind to others?

A woman speaks 5,000 more words than a man. Remember a man speaks in headlines (give him the bullet points) and a woman speaks in stories (she wants the details)

Ever listen, really listen to some people talk? So many useless words, everyone listening to respond and no one listening to understand. You leave the conversation exhausted or hurt for that matter.

There are fast talkers, who speak so fast to confuse you, there are word-fillers "like", "you know what I mean"...the world is a noisy place, some people talk just to hear themselves speak. Words can confuse you, lead you, and break you. Verbal abuse is damaging to one's spirit.

Children grow up with parents who never say I love you, you are beautiful, what a handsome young man you are. Instead, all they hear is you are useless, you will never grow up to be anything good.

My heart aches for these children, they need to hear they are loved and have blessings spoken over them, instead of curses.

Imagine a world filled with less noise, less words and people using them to uplift others. Giving affirmation rather then put downs. Using positivity rather than negative. Reading the Bible and knowing what God feels, thinks and says about you.

Sadness falls away to joy, pain gives way to healing and love abounds! Yes Lord, give me more of You and let my flesh die out.

Only you can control that one muscle in your mouth. Use it for good! Listen more, speak less and when you do speak let it be to edify.

Proverbs 11:17 "Your own soul is nourished when you are kind, but you destroy yourself when you are cruel." Proverbs 15: 1 "A gentle answer turns away wrath, but hard words stir up anger." Proverbs 15:4 "Gentle words bring life and health; a deceitful tongue crushes the spirit."

Ever notice how we judge or criticize others or even ourselves. Watch carefully what comes out of your mouth, our words are containers of power. Ever notice what you judge or criticize is what you don't like within yourself?

Matthew 7:5...pull the plank out of your own eye.

We need to be more concerned about that speck in us and work in making ourselves the best that we can be so that when we run into that person we want to judge, we can change our response and reaction to one of love and perhaps being a vessel that God put that person there for you to minister to.

Our criticizing does damage to us as well, we find fault with, censure, denounce, condemn, attack, lambaste, disapprove of, cast aspersions on, pour scorn on, disparage, deprecate, malign, vilify, and run down. These words are powerful and not of love.

Next time you want to criticize someone or even yourself think of the words above. Do you really want to give power to disparage or condemn others or yourself with the power of your words?

We become what we judge and criticize. Change your mindset, change your world.

The world has lost itself, everything that was good is now bad and everything bad is now good.

An upside-down world on fire. We criticize in judgmental ways; we shame someone for having an opinion that is different than yours and everyone is about to explode.

(Matthew 7:1). Rather than judging others, we should observe and correct our own shortcomings and sin. It is a waste of our time and energy to judge others while we could focus on improving ourselves.

Could you imagine a world of people focusing on correcting themselves! To look at themselves and ask why do I dislike this person? What is it about them that rubs me the wrong way?

Turn the mirror and look at yourself, you may find the answer. Perhaps, that's why you don't seek the answer because you don't want to know the truth about you.

In the healing journey, (and we never stop, life is a learning journey) I teach the women to alway challenge themselves with those self-questions.

1 Corinthians 5:10 "not at all meaning the people of this world who are immoral, or the greedy and swindlers, or idolaters.

The Bible has a lot to say on judging and criticism, in short...don't.

John 8:7 When they kept on questioning him, he straightened up and said to them, "Let any one of you who is without sin be the first to throw a stone at her."

If we are without blemish then throw the stone, but none of us are without blemish or sin. We all, every one of us are sinners so next time you want to judge read the verse below:

Luke 6:37 Judge not, and ye shall not be judged: condemn not, and ye shall not be condemned: forgive, and ye shall be forgiven.

If we are dead to sin, then it will lose its power over us. If we are alive to God, we will respond in love and obedience to his Word and his Spirit.

Father, forgive me, change me Lord.

Life seems like everything is ending. The winter season has been around for too long. Just like a season, it too must end and new things begin to bud as spring come after winter.

But winter is an important season for life. Don't shortchange your season of winter, learn from it, plan your days and before you know it, the days get lighter and buds begin to show themselves.

It's been a long winter season for everyone with isolation, but if you turn your perspective around and ask what can I learn from this season in my life; you will ready yourself for new opportunities.

Lamentations 3:22-23, "The steadfast love of the Lord never ceases; his mercies never come to an end; they are new every morning; great is your faithfulness."

Matthew 5:16, "In the same way, let your light shine before others, so that they may see your good works and give glory to your Father who is in heaven."

There comes a point in your life when you realize who matters, who never did, who won't anymore and who always will.

So, don't worry about people from your past, there's a reason why they didn't make it to your future.

A season and a reason and always a lesson. Learn from them.

Who are you? If I asked you this question, would you give me resume answers? I'm a hardworking, detailed, organized person. Or would you give me your personality traits, I am a type A person, or how about your behaviors?

Those are not who are you, they are what you do. To your very core, who are you? Your identity? I am a child of God 1st; my identity lies within my foundation built on solid rock...I am a child of God.

Where are you? Would your answer be, I am sad, I am blessed or I am happy? Or will you be truthful I am stuck in pain? Where is your identity?

Where do you want to be in 3 months, six month or 1 year from now? List your goals, do a vision board, expand your territory. A goal in your head, stays in your head; a goal written down becomes a plan. Work that plan and lay your petitions before the Lord. Sell yourself to yourself!

Don't sit still, don't go backwards. Fatigue breeds fatigue; exercise breeds energy. A body in motion stays in motion. Keep your body flexible and your mind sharp.

It's time for full immersion, to apply all that you have learned. Who influences you? Who are your close 5? Do they influence good and positive or complaining and negative?

Each morning God gives us a new beginning, a chance to do something different. What will you do with this wonderful opportunity? Continue to do old things? There is nothing new there. Move forward, without change, growth is impossible.

Begin preparing your land to sow good seed. You and your mind, spirit and body is that land. Prepare it for good stuff. What is holding you back? I want to move and start a new life! You take yourself where ever you go. God gives you the chance to write a new story every morning. Don't bring your broken piece into your new story.

God wants Kingdom thinkers, kingdom vessels that He can work through. It is not all about you. When you come outside yourself to be of service to someone, you take your eyes off of your circumstances (horizontal thinking) and it is the best feeling to help someone. God is Spirit and needs Kingdom vessels. Make a list of some people you can help. It is not always money. What about a neighbor? A co-worker?

There is no greater satisfaction than hearing the words...well done my good and faithful servant from the One I keep my faith in.

Thank you Lord Jesus for your continued Grace and Mercy. May I continue to be a vessel that you can work through. It's not about me. It's all about You.

Many of you know me and my struggles and some of you joined my page from all over the world looking for healing and hope. I pray it has been a source of comfort.

The past 14 days COVID-19 has invaded my husband and my body, a thief in the night attacking our strength, mind and bodies. In a weakened state, my writings have dwindled as brain fog has been a struggle.

I write this not for sympathy but as a learning experience that if you are weak, He is strong. We must remind ourselves to lean not on our own understanding. In all things (sickness too) to go to the Source and lean on Him.

Our hope cannot be in anyone but our Lord and Savior. When we misplace that, we are disappointed and our life goes out of spiral. God doesn't leave us; He is for you!

Remind yourself who you are. Straightened your crowns, Kings and Queens. You are a child of the Creator.

Keep your eyes on Christ Jesus. Sometimes when walking in the dry desert land, when you can't see or hear Him; we have to remind ourselves He will never leave us or forsake us.

Where is He when everything around us is in chaos? Isiah 58:11 says "And the Lord will continually guide you,
And satisfy your desire in scorched places,
And give strength to your bones; And you will be like a watered garden, and like a spring of water whose waters do not fail."

These are the times where we need to be like King David and encourage ourselves in the Lord. Though I can't see You or feel You, I know You are there...faith, big faith during the times of drought.

We need to press even further into His word. Like the time of drought, the trees roots will press even further into the ground to find the water. Yes! Be like a tree roots press in.

Luke 11:24 "When the unclean spirit goes out of a man, it passes through waterless places seeking rest, and not finding any, it says, 'I will return to my house from which I came."

Isiah 1:30 For you will be like an oak whose leaf fades away or as a garden that has no water."

Encourage yourself in the Lord when you hit those dry places in your journey. He is for you!

In a day, you get 24 hours. What will you do with them? Mindlessly scroll through (not so social) media?

Or create a day of progress, a day where you plan a time to wake, a time to give thanks to the Lord, a time to walk with Him and talk with Him?

Creating a list and putting exercise, reading, errands, and all thing things you need to accomplish, puts those goals into a plan.

A person without vision perishes. And the Lord answered me: "Write the vision; make it plain on tablets, so he may run who reads it." Where there is no prophetic vision, the people cast off restraint, but blessed is he who keeps the law. For still the vision awaits its appointed time; it hastens to the end—it will not lie. Habakkuk 2:2

The thought stays in your mind, a goal written down becomes a plan, the plan on a board becomes a vision.

Proverbs 21:5 "The plans of the diligent lead to profit as surely as haste leads to poverty."

Proverbs 24:27 "Put your outdoor work in order and get your fields ready; after that, build your house."

Proverbs 29:18 "Where there is no vision, the people are unrestrained, but happy is he who keeps the law."

What is your vision? What is your plan? Don't have one? This morning is a new day to begin.

Doubt can be cast over or on something or someone. It can happen with just speaking certain words that can be throwed forcefully (casting).

Our words are powerful, loose lips sink ships, or have the power to destroy a life, that someone took a life-time to build. Our words cast a shadow over that person and it can damage them for years or for that matter their lifetime.

Today, so many words are spoken by us, in jest, to destroy, to gossip, to give your opinion (we all have them) and want to respond.

An average man speaks 7,000 words in the course of a day, an average woman speaks 20,000 words in one day, some speak much more than that. Of your 7,000 -20,000 words you will use today; how many of them will be used to help, uplift and be kind to others?

A woman speaks 5,000 more words than a man. Remember a man speaks in headlines (give him the bullet points) and a woman speaks in stories (she wants the details)

Ever listen, really listen to some people talk? So many useless words, everyone listening to respond and no one listening to understand. You leave the conversation exhausted or hurt for that matter.

There are fast talkers, who speak so fast to confuse you, there are word-fillers "like", "you know what I mean"...the world is a noisy place, some people talk just to hear themselves speak. Words can confuse you, lead you, and break you. Verbal abuse is damaging to one's spirit.

Children grow up with parents who never say I love you, you are beautiful, what a handsome young man you are. Instead, all they hear is you are useless, you will never grow up to be anything good. My heart aches for these children, they need to hear they are loved and have blessings spoken over them, instead of curses.

Imagine a world filled with less noise, less words and people using them to uplift others. Giving affirmation rather then put downs. Using positivity rather than negative. Reading the Bible and knowing what God feels, thinks and says about you.

Sadness falls away to joy, pain gives way to healing and love abounds! Yes Lord, give me more of You and let my flesh die out.

Only you can control that one muscle in your mouth. Use it for good! Listen more, speak less and when you do speak let it be to edify.

Proverbs 11:17 "Your own soul is nourished when you are kind, but you destroy yourself when you are cruel." Proverbs 15: 1 "A gentle answer turns away wrath, but hard words stir up anger." Proverbs 15:4 "Gentle words bring life and health; a deceitful tongue crushes the spirit."

Seeing each other in a different light (perspective).

"Take Mark...he is profitable...for the ministry." 2 Timothy 4:11

Who are your close 5? Your tribe? Do they influence you the right way...are they profitable to you, no not money, but influence? Or do 1 or 2 bring you down with each conversation or visit?

Do you surround yourself with yes friends? Or do you like the ones that will tell you the truth out of love?

"We have this treasure in earthen vessels." 2 Col 4:7

Do you motivate that treasure, or do you devalue it? You can't expect you from everyone.

Influence, motivate, extend grace and mercy and forgiveness.

They come for a season, learn from it and a reason, and find out your why.

You may have been called a different way. Seek 1st the things of God. Let's be Kingdom minded. Extend kindness, grace and forgiveness.

"One who has unreliable friends soon comes to ruin, but there is a friend who sticks closer than a brother." "A friend loves at all times, and a brother is born for a time of adversity." ... "My intercessor is my friend as my eyes pour out tears to God; on behalf of a man, he pleads with God as one pleads for a friend." Proverbs 18:24

The Bible talks about strife, but what is strife: angry or bitter disagreement over fundamental issues; conflict. Philippians 2:3 says, let nothing be done through strife.

When we are angry and our anger turns into bitterness, our actions and words will come out ugly, hurtful and bitter to those around us. Hurt people, hurt people.

Don't let your emotions control you. You are in control of them, if you're not you need to be. Decisions should never be made when you are emotional.

Strive causes chaos in churches, relationships, marriages and even business. Jas 3:16 says "Where envy and strife is, there is... every evil work."

So, the Bible is saying evil prevails through strife and envy.

We are to be in control of ourselves, our response and stay away from strife and envy. Hebrews 12:15 says "See...no root of bitterness springing up, causes trouble..."

God's blessing cannot be upon us if we are in conflict of His word. So, forgive those who have hurt you. Speak blessings over them, pray for them so that your Father in heaven can pour out His Blessings upon you.

Learn how to control your emotions. Is it easy to do? No, but the sooner you learn how to, the more at peace you become and learn silence speaks louder at times than a hurtful word.

We want to snuff out pain, not feel the effects of it, sometimes disabling pain. But our pain is there to teach us and to alert us, something needs our attention. So, to try and drown out the pain with pills or alcohol only dulls it, it's still there once the artificial pain killer wears off.

Ask yourself what is this pain trying to tell me. If it is physical pain, perhaps your body is saying...get up and move your body. Perhaps it saying you have too much sugar inside and it's crying out...please eat better. Listen to your body, it has a defense system, you only need to listen to it.

There are so many types of pain; pain from surgery, pain from a breakup, emotional pain...and the list goes on. If we stop, dig deep and listen to our body we can come up with natural defenses to combat the pain.

DISCLAIMER-go to the doctor, in no way do you ignore pain. This is speaking to emotional pain.

Pain again is there to alert us; it is our barometer that something needs our attention. Don't mask it, go and find the answers to gain through your pain.

It could be gripping fear, anxiety, worry or a panic attack. Our worry places great undue stress on our body.

Next time you feel like you are fighting just to get through another day, remember Satan hasn't snatch the steering wheel from God. God is still in control. Encourage yourself in the Lord. Victory is born out of struggle.

What is your pain trying to get your attention? Name it, give it your Healer Jesus Christ.

Fear, anxiety, worry, depression, these are the feelings of almost every American. What does the future hold? Where are we going as a nation divided? Am I going to lose my job, my house, or my car?

Be anxious for nothing, tomorrow will take care of itself. Easy to say, hard to do right. If you change your paradigm by living in the moment and not assume about tomorrow, you can learn not to live in the "what if's".

No one wants to lose their home or car, but okay, what if you did? God as your Provider will replace the things the enemy has stolen with something new or better.

This is where faith comes in, the faith of a mustard seed (which is very small). Therefore, the more you exercise your faith the bigger it gets. Like the woman who crawled in a crowd of thousands, just to touch the hem of Jesus garment. Matthew 9:21

Imagine, "If I can just touch the hem of his garment, I will be healed." This was said by a broken woman who was looking for healing. Bleeding for 12 years, she was considered an outcast. Due to her condition, she was not allowed into the temple, nor was she allowed to touch another person. So, she crawled, with her faith so large that she knew, she would be healed.

Stand boldly before fear, anxiety, worry, and tell them to get thee behind you in Jesus's name. Knowing that He is your Healer, He is your Provider, that He is your Way-Maker.

When something bad happens, go vertical. When something good happens, go vertical and give thanks.

When your prayers are answered, go vertical...in all things give Him all the Glory and Praise for He alone is Worthy.

That same Power that raised the dead, the same Power that split the Red Sea...is still here with us, through His Holy Spirit. Greater is He in us, then he who is in this world.

Going vertical (praying looking up). He is always Powerful; He is still in Control. God, I trust You, Jesus my Lord and Savior.

Keep trusting (your faith), keep asking (your petitions) and keep going to Him. I trust you Lord Jesus in all things.

Go vertical and watch your life change. Yes, prayer changes everything.

Did you know that control stems from that person's insecurities? We are talking about someone's need to control a situation or spouse (not position at work).

The definition of control is the power to make decisions about how something is managed or done. The ability to direct the actions of someone or something.

Domestic abuse, mind games from a narcissistic person, uses control to ensure the outcome for them. At first, it is subtle and then overtime it increases until they are controlling the person.

The victim at 1st may think, "oh they love me" but overtime when they increase the control, it could morph into violence. Be on the lookout for the red flags, the verbal assault, the 1st time they tell you what to wear, how to clean and if they begin the 1st signs of restraining you (not allowing you to leave a room or a slap). More than likely it will be followed by, "I'm sorry, I'll never do it again", until it is followed by, "look at what you made me do".

I use they and not he because it could be the woman too.

Three basic types of control systems are available to executives: (1) output control, (2) behavioral control, and (3) clan control.

We are talking about #2. The controller conditions you over time to be controlled. Sounds scary? It is domestic abuse is one of the most violent crimes.

Reach out for help, there are so many great organizations that can help you.

Beware of false prophets, which come to you in sheep's clothing, but inwardly they are ravening wolves. Matthew 7:15

The enemy used to hide in the darkness, today he is out in the open and we still don't recognize him. Contact is dangerous, particularly false teachers and the false prophets.

Who are you listening to? Is it contrary to the Bible?

You shall have no other gods before me. This is expressed in the Bible in Exodus 20:3, Matthew 4:10, Luke 4:8 and elsewhere, e.g.: Ye shall make you no idols nor graven image, neither rear you up a standing image, neither shall ye set up any image of stone in your land, to bow down unto it: for I am the Lord your God.

How many idols do you set before God? Social media? God 1st in all things. Try it, pray for your day in the morning. Give God some of your time and watch the Peace and the Joy of the Lord enter your days.

Palestine removed all the Blacksmith's from Israel. Why, so they could not make swords for them to defend themselves. The Bible says; "There were no blacksmiths in the land." 1 Samuel 13:19.

The Philistine's wanted to keep the Israelites in slavery. What a devastating blow to a nation to not be able to defend itself, to silence them, a kingdom nation.

It's time for us to be Kingdom minded. Calling upon all spiritual blacksmiths to mold and shape our spiritual swords.

Ephesians 6:12: "For we wrestle not against flesh and blood, but against principalities, against powers, against the rulers of the darkness of this world, against spiritual wickedness in high places"

"And take the helmet of salvation, and the sword of the Spirit, which is the word of God." Ephesians 6:17

We all have a God-given gift of discernment. It is a gift of knowing between right and wrong, good and evil and truth and false.

We can discern more with our spirit than we can with our eyes.1 John 2:20 "You have an unction from the Holy One, and you know all things." God will let you know things. Some of us discern more than others because we listen with our spirit. Our eyes can be deceiving.

Take a spider for instance, they have 8 eyes but their vision is bad. They see through feeling through their legs. We should learn to see more through our gift of discernment.

Ever meet someone and your eyes say one thing, but your spirit gives off warning signals? "His anointing teaches...whether something is real or counterfeit...1Jn 2:27.

Learning to discern and walk closer to Him is learning to walk in the Kingdom.

Proverbs 30:28 "The spider takes hold with her hands, and is in the kings palace."

You've heard the saying marriage is 50-50. This couldn't be further from the truth. Marriage is giving 100% each. It is work, but the more you give, the more you get. Like good soil, you have to work the land, till the ground and then seed and water it. Only then can you watch it grow.

Too often, 1 person does all the work and becomes emotionally drained and sits it out. Their emotional bank account is drained.

If you have both of the couple working at it at the same time... oh what a beautiful field of flowers you will have. An emotional bank account that is full, so when 1 needs to withdraw from it... there is plenty.

Next time you feel drained, make sure you both make a deposit into a good account...your marriage.

We have been given the authority through Christ Jesus to anoint.

The purpose of anointing with the holy anointing oil is to sanctify, to set the anointed person or object apart as "holy" (Exodus 30:29).

This means our homes too...do you, or have you cleansed your home? Anointed your car or vehicles? Your children for His Blessings upon them?

What! My car, yes, asking the Lord to surround your car to protect it from any accident or harm that would try to come up against it.

Ephesians 6:16, "Above all, taking the shield of faith, wherewith ye shall be able to quench all the fiery darts of the wicked."

It might be a flaming arrow of fear, or a flaming arrow of impure thoughts, or an arrow of fear. But God tells us to fear not, that He is always there to protect us. We need to do the things the Bible gives us power and authority over.

Get your oil and begin taking that authority over your home, your vehicles and your healing. Tell fear he must flee in Jesus's name. Be bold, stand in what has been given to you as an heir in the Kingdom of God!

Everything that Jesus wants to get done on earth today, He does it through us, believers in His name, who we have been given the Power of Attorney to act on His behalf.

February is the second month in the year, but it is the last month of winter. Since February of 2020, the world has been stymied into a winter season. Like all seasons they are meant to change... your season is about to manifest some fruit. Let this winter teach you a valuable lesson.

If you are quarantined inside your home make lists of things to do today. Keep your mind active...read.

Stretching, moving your body fatigue breeds fatigue; exercise breeds energy. Don't like to exercise, stretching, balancing and flap your arms, is still a body in motion. The Egoscue Method is great for getting the body to move, bend and stretch. A body in motion stays in motion. You are creating energy in your body.

...but those who hope in the Lord will renew their strength. They will soar on wings like eagles; they will run and not grow weary; they will walk and not be faint. Isaiah 40:31

"I'm too tired" is one of the most common excuses not to exercise out there. Change your perspective on exercise. Say stretching instead, say dancing, do anything to get your energy level up. That alone changes your brain chemistry into happy brain.

Remember a seed goes into the ground first and is covered in darkness. Begin to water yourself, you've been in darkness for too long. It's time to spring forth and show your buds.

Want your springtime to come early? Start preparing the groundwork...your mind. If you worked on a farm you would have to prepare the land. Your body, soul and mind, is your land...let's prep it for the spring season, it's been a long winter.

Listen to inspirational music, or allow yourself to just listen to the sound of nature around you. Go for a walk, especially if you can spend time in nature. God is for you; He's just waiting for you to begin.

Are you moving forward or are you stationary? The definition of stationary is not intended to move, not changing in quantity or condition.

If a staircase is in front of you and the only way of getting in, is by climbing the staircase, would you?

This doesn't mean you have to move by you selling your home and move to another state. But it does mean with God, He gives you free-will, choices but if you make the wrong choice; don't blame God.

Remember the game "Let's Make a Deal" the host would say choice door 1-2 or 3 and just as you are about to choose, he tempts you with another choice; I have here in my pocket an envelope; it could contain 10,000.00. Make a choice!

Life is that way, do I sell, do I buy, do I leave my job, do I stay? Make the wrong choice and it can be devastating.

But with prayer and supplication (asking earnestly) for Jesus to take the wheel; Father God, Your Will be done...now that there, is the right move...pray. If it's not His Will, I don't want it.

He will make a way and it will go smoothly and He will give you everything you need. Move too quickly, get ahead of Him can have devastating effects.

If you seek His Will and go according to His plan you will have everything you will need. He has already made a way for you.

In all things ask that His Will be done!

We serve a forward moving God. His creation was never meant to be stagnant, flowers bloom, they drop seed, bees pollinate them and the grow and expand. Are you moving forward or stuck?

Genesis 9:7 "And you, be fruitful and multiply, increase greatly on the earth and multiply in it."

He wanted us to not only multiply in numbers but to subdue the land; conquer, defeat, overcome, and control the land.

Has the weariness of the world crushed your spirit, your will, your dreams?

When God lead the Israelites out into the wilderness they grumbled and complained...manna, manna, manna...where was their leeks and food they enjoyed in Egypt.

Has God moved you forward to learn a new thing and you are stuck in your past grumbling? His plan is to move you beyond surviving to thriving, but He can't bless the complaining.

When God moves you to unfamiliar places, it's time to take off the training wheels, learn something new and learn your new places.

You were not meant to stand still, you were meant to grow and expand not to just survive. Stop having a victim, or slave mentality and have a thriving in the Kingdom attitude.

Take off your old self and put on a new self. The winter season is almost over. Spring is about to start...what new thing will you do?

Create a compelling future by setting realistic goals but set the bar higher for yourself.

Today we are all told what to do. We are all called to disciple, to help one another.

Who are you?
What is your identity?
Train your physical self, energy begets energy, fatigue begets fatigue.

Get excited about your life. Write a new story, delete the old ones, there's nothing new in your past. You write your story through your identity; what do you focus on?

If you are expecting someone to rescue you; you could be waiting a long time. The government, friends or even family will save you.

You and God alone; "He will give you another Counselor" John 14:16

In the Bible, Solomon lists twenty-eight different seasons in life:

Here they are: "A time to be born and a time to die. A time to plant and a time to harvest. A time to kill and a time to heal. A time to tear down and a time to build up. A time to cry and a time to laugh. A time to grieve and a time to dance. A time to scatter stones and a time to gather stones. A time to embrace and a time to turn away. A time to search and a time to quit searching. A time to keep and a time to throw away. A time to tear and a time to mend. A time to be quiet and a time to speak. A time to love and a time to hate. A time for war and a time for peace" (Ecc 3:2-8 NLT).

God determines each of your life's seasons. The Psalmist said, "My times are in thy hand" (Ps 31:15). So, what should you do when you enter a new season of life? Reach for the Holy Spirit's help because He's your "Counselor." Jesus told His disciples, "I will ask the Father, and he will give you another Counselor to be with you forever." When you need an advisor because you're not sure what to do or which way to go, the Holy Spirit is available to guide you. That means you must be sensitive when He highlights a particular Scripture you're reading, or plants a persistent thought or idea in your mind that won't go away, or speaks to you through a friend. You're not alone, unless you want to be. Just consult the "Counselor" within you.

Today, is a new day, winter will be over soon and spring will reveal things that were buried. What will you do with this blessing?

In group last week, we spoke about "what if", too many of us live there...what if I lose my job, what if I lose my house. Last night, we spoke about living in the "what is", living in the moment.

We can't change the what if's, but we can change our thought process to living in what is, right now and trusting God to take care of our tomorrow. That doesn't mean we sit back and do nothing. We are here and now; we need to set goals and plan for our future. But don't get stuck in the "what if's".

Matthew 6:25-27 "Therefore, I tell you, do not worry about your life, what you will eat or drink; or about your body, what you will wear. Is not life more than food, and the body more than clothes? Look at the birds of the air; they do not sow or reap or store away in barns, and yet your heavenly Father feeds them. Are you not much more valuable than they? Can any one of you by worrying add a single hour to your life.

Can any one of you add a single hour to your life by worrying? No, worry leads to anxiety and anxiety leads to stress and stress leads to body ailments.

Change your thoughts and live in "what is", living in the present. What was is past, what if, hasn't happened and what is, is right now.

Seek God and His Kingdom. Go about doing Kingdom work. Go to the Comforter for help and keep your eyes vertical.

What "if", what "is" and what "was". Today, let's discuss what "was". Most of us either live in what was, or what if, one has already happened and the other hasn't. The one thing they have in common is you can't change either of them. But what if you can change your response, attitude and the path that you take, therefore being an active participant in your "what if".

What was can torment you with pain and the thoughts of it; If I could only change this. But once that second has passed, it becomes your past. Once that stone is thrown, or word spoken, there is no taking it back.

Have you ever opened your mouth and as the words were coming out you realized, I shouldn't have said that. You wished you could grab them from the air before they reached the ears of the listener? I have!

However, you have already cast that stone and you can't take it back.

We are creatures of habit, without even thinking we do things out of routine or habit. Can we change the past? No, but we can change our habits that create bad "what was" for our future. Wrong choices that we do again and again, sometimes expecting a different result (this is the definition of insanity) and we, yes you drive yourself insane.

Exercise: clasp your hands together, intertwine your fingers. Which thumb is on top of the other one? Usually a right-handed person, your right thumb would be on top.

Now, break your hands apart and try it the other way (left thumb on top). Feels weird, right? Right-handed people will begin to brush their teeth on the left side of their mouth. Today, without thinking about it, which side did you begin?

We can train our minds to do and learn a new thing. Try for a week to brush your teeth different each day.

At first, there will be a rub, a weird feeling, but as your brain adapts, you learn a new way. It is as simple as that even with more complex habits. Give yourself the gift of change and growth every day, but by doing something different on purpose.

Don't allow "what was" to rob you of "what is"; today is a gift, a new beginning...what will you write on your blank page? The same thing as yesterday(s), or with Christ all things become new!

Be in control of your mind, be in control of your emotions and be in control of your words. If we are not in control of these things, we can become a loose cannon that just fires off at the wrong time.

Ever hear the old adage loose lips sink ships? Although Loose lips sink ships is an American English idiom meaning "beware of unguarded talk". The phrase originated on propaganda posters during World War II. The phrase was created by the War Advertising Council and used on posters by the United States Office of War Information. Some words are warring words.

Your mind is where it begins and it flows so freely out of some mouths. Some just can't seem to help it, the words just keep coming out.

Yesterday, we spoke about bringing every thought captive, today, is to think before speaking. Listen to understand. Don't listen to respond. Once the words leave your mouth, you cannot take them back. They have made it to the listeners ears, went deep into their soul and they are left with processing what you said.

Society today, hides behind their keyboards using so many words to destroy, to tear down and in some cases to kill...a reputation or bullying. This my friend is not of God.

Bring every thought captive (in your mind), think before you respond. The Bible says that a fool can be recognized by his many words (Ecclesiastes 5:3).

Ecclesiastes 10:14 adds that a fool "multiplies words. A fool talk too much? The Bible discourages using an abundance of words where a few words would suffice.

"Even fools are thought wise if they keep silent, and discerning if they hold their tongues" (Proverbs 17:28). Those who feel compelled to give utterance to every thought in their heads. You know a few of these, maybe you might be one yourself?

Proverbs 10:19 warns that talking too much naturally leads to sin: "When words are many, transgression is not lacking, but whoever restrains his lips is prudent".

The wise person refuses to talk too much. Rather, he fears the Lord, listens to the Lord, and obeys the Lord. He follows the example of Mary, "who sat at the Lord's feet listening to what he said" (Luke 10:39).

When our mouths are full of our own words, we have little time or interest in God's words. Talking too much usually means listening too little, or just listening to respond, cutting others off so that you can speak is not listening.

What a wonderful awesome book the Bible is. So much wisdom given to us pointing the way for us to learn and live. If you have seen yourself in the above, change the way you listen and respond.

Listen to understand the one speaking, what do you hear? Don't think about what your response is, think about what they are really saying...sometimes it is not the words spoken, but the unspoken.

Challenge: listen all day to understand the speaker.

What are you battling today? We all are battling something; sickness, financial, depression, selfishness, boredom...the list goes on.

1 Corinthians 10:24 "Nobody should seek his own good, but the good of others".

The definition of battle is "a sustained fight between large organized armed forces." Battling the above is a sustained fight. To war against these things, how do you battle?

Jesus gives us the way, the truth and our blueprint to arm us during these battles. Put on the full armor of God.

When He was on the cross, He took time for the criminal hanging on the cross next to Him. Imagine the pain and suffering He felt, but He took His eyes off Himself. (Luke 23:39-43).

When Stephen was being stoned to death, he prayed for those who were killing him, can you imagine that. He asked God not to lay the sin to their charge (Acts 7:59-60) self-less-ness...are you?

When you are in the midst of your battle, do you become selfish, or come outside of your circumstances and pour out to someone else?

When we come outside ourselves to help another, we remove our eyes off of our circumstance and God rewards with His Blessings.

How many would you possibly lead to His Kingdom if you showed His Love rather than judging, rejection, or criticism? Being in control of our emotions.

Next time, self-indulgence wants to come in, turn it around to selflessness and see who you can help. Be truthful, especially to yourself what is it that you are doing to help advance the Kingdom of God?

Go light your world. Be a blessing, the world needs more of this!

The battle of our minds is the most difficult to overcome. We've spoken about being in control of our emotions, which I feel are easier to overcome. But the battle of the mind, which controls habits, behavior, and your body. Yes, here is the real war we must fight to overcome.

Our mind is powerful and can conjure up more than what is truly before us. We can have a thought and it can go wild in our minds (much like the picture below), we make a mountain out of an ant hill.

For the weapons of our warfare are not carnal but mighty in God for pulling down strongholds, casting down arguments and every high thing that exalts itself against the knowledge of God, bringing every thought into captivity to the obedience of Christ. '' 2 Corinthians 10:4-5.

Casting down arguments...throughout the New Testament, did you ever hear Jesus argue? When He spoke, everyone listened.

High thing that exalts itself against the knowledge of God, we do this especially if we do not bring every thought captive.

Our weapons are mighty in God for the pulling down of strongholds. Here is where we fight our battles.

In our Healing Hearts sessions we learn not to assume, ask clarifying questions and that silence sometimes speaks louder than words.

Today, I challenge you to try the scripture above. It will be hard, but once you have mastered this, your world will change, especially you.

"But if it is buried, it sprouts and reproduces...many times over."
Jn 12:25

God created you to flourish: (1) Your relationships. Relationally, your languishing self is often troubled.

You're undisciplined in what you say, sometimes reverting to sarcasm, gossip, and flattery. You isolate. You dominate. You attack. You withdraw.

Whereas your flourishing self seeks to bless others. They energize you. You're able to disclose your thoughts and feelings in a way that invites openness in them. You're quick to admit your own mistakes, and to freely forgive others.

(2) Your experiences: God grows you because He wants to use you in His plans to redeem His world: That's why you find Him changing your experiences. Your flourishing self has a desire to contribute. You live with a sense of calling.

Indeed, your inner longing to become all you were meant to be is a tiny echo of God's longing to begin the new creation.

The rabbi's spoke of this astikkun olam—to repair the world. Focused on yourself, your life is as small as a grain of wheat. Given to God, however, it's as if that grain is planted in rich soil, growing into part of a much bigger project.

Jesus said: "Unless a grain of wheat is buried in the ground, dead to the world, it is never any more than a grain of wheat. But if it is buried, it sprouts and reproduces...many times over. John 12:24

In the same way, anyone who holds on to life ...as it is destroys that life. But if you let it go, reckless in your love, you'll have it forever, real and eternal. John 12:25

Keep growing, don't stop learning, like a seed goes into the ground covered by darkness. Soak up the nutrients in the ground and break your way into the light. We learn in the dark place; we grow and sprout forth in the light.

King Solomon was a wise king. He gave 28 different seasons we as humans or for that matter life, plants everything has a life cycle.

We should seize the opportunity that God gives us here on earth, now. Nothing can stop this appointed time to live or die. You were appointed this generation to be born. Not the 1700's or the 1900's, now this time.

Too many of us dwell or live in the past. Or some of us are stuck on the future "what if", the only thing we have is what is, right here and now. No matter how hard we try, we can't avoid that we are here now.

Isn't it time to put the past where it belongs? You can't change it, you can only change now and future. What path will you choose?

Which season are you in today? There are 28 that King Solomon gave:

Ecclesiastes 3:2-8 NLT "A time to be born and a time to die. A time to plant and a time to harvest. A time to kill and a time to heal. A time to tear down and a time to build up. A time to cry and a time to laugh. A time to grieve and a time to dance. A time to scatter stones and a time to gather stones. A time to embrace and a time to turn away. A time to search and a time to quit searching. A time to keep and a time to throw away. A time to tear and a time to mend. A time to be quiet and a time to speak. A time to love and a time to hate. A time for war and a time for peace."

Choose wisely for tomorrow hasn't happened yet, yesterday is over and today choose joy, laughter, healing, dancing and peace.

Philippians 4:6 "And the peace that surpasses all understanding will guard your hearts and minds in Christ Jesus."

There are always layers of feelings. When you name them and begin peeling them back like an onion, you expose the next and next until you get to the core reason.

Naming those emotions helps you identify the real reason you are frustrated. Why are you frustrated, oh this client just made me angry? What was it that that got you angry? I just got mad.

Frustrated lead to anger, anger leads to mad. Now that these 3 levels have been identified you can get to what made you mad.

Remorseful can lead to feelings of guilt to feeling sad when you peel those layers back and realize perhaps you had something to do with it. No shame, God does not bring condemnation upon you. He only convicts our spirit to feel remorse so we can come to a place of forgiveness.

So, before you become apathetic, lonely or depressed, let it go to the One who forgives all. Ask Him, lord forgive me for I have sinned. His yoke is easy His shoulders are large enough to take your burdens.

Go deep beyond the surface and dig out that root cause and leave it at the foot of the cross. Cast out loneliness, cast out sadness, cast out depression in Jesus's name. This is not of God. He gives you Joy and Peace.

Remember your faith, remember that feeling I can do all things through Christ who strengthens me.

Remember the days when you prayed and just believe as the words were exiting your mouth to God's ears, He heard you and would say yes and amen.

When you were 1st saved did you believe He was answering your prayers? Or did it take you a while to grow the kind of faith...if I can just touch the hem of His garment?

No matter what you are going through, Jesus is the same, it is you that changes, or your faith waivers or grows...I just know everything I pray He hears me. I pray with expectation that the Great I Am, hears me.

He knows my needs before I utter them. I lay my petitions before him, then I thank Him for them, that they are coming my way. Praying with expectation.

Matthew 21:22 And whatever you ask in prayer, you will receive, if you have faith."

Mark 9:29 And he said to them, "This kind cannot be driven out by anything but prayer."

Mark 11:24 Therefore, I tell you, whatever you ask in prayer, believe that you have received it, and it will be yours.

He give us our prescription right there on how to pray.

Step 1 - Abide in Christ the Vine.
Step 2 - Pray in Faith.
Step 3 - Stand on God's Word.
Step 4 - Pray in the Spirit.
Step 5 - Persevere in Prayer.
Step 6 - Use Different Types of Prayer.
Step 7 - Flow in God's Love.

There you have it! Go ahead He's listening...Father God, you are Worthy, I thank you for listening... (lay your petitions here) in Jesus' name. Amen

Ever seen someone so broken they walk with their head down? When they talk, they advert their eyes from meeting yours? They may give you a second smile that isn't real because there is nothing in their life to smile about. Their self-worth is so shattered, they are in so much pain. On the inside they are screaming "Don't you see the hurt and pain".

Many of them won't make it out of their darkness, like sinking further into a dark well, the light above shrinks with each day that they fall another level into the dark abyss.

This darkness is no longer depression, it is a whole other level of bondage, hopelessness and pain. Thoughts of suicide enter in and now this is the only escape to them...suicide.

What if I told you there is hope? There is another way, but it will take commitment and work to get to the other side and application. Like putting on your clothes, you will have to take what you learn and apply it daily to your life. On the other side is Love, Empowerment, Worth and finding yourself again. Would you take it?

I am a walking testimony of God's Goodness and Grace; His Love and Mercy for you.

Healing your heart is a journey, but one worth it...finding you!

In the six years of doing Healing Hearts, I have witnessed God's Healing Power and seen women get healed. It is beautiful!

That moment when you hear the news, your 1st reaction is denial... no it can't be! Like seeing an accident, you can't look away, your stomach feels ill and your heart grips as it beats faster. Can it be?

Emotions come flooding in, you don't know where to turn, your mind is racing with thoughts flooding in like waters about to overtake you. You feel like you are in a rubber dingy and you are paddling as fast as you can...but you are drowning in thought.

You want to scream, cry, and instead you just sit wondering what to do...you are broken, hurt and shattered by the news. Your thoughts turn to you, what could I have done? Was it me? When did this happen? How could I have not noticed.

Then come after the denial, hurt and shattering/pain...comes anger. I'm going to stop here, because this is where you need to stop as well. The anger can morph into depression, addiction and so many other dark feelings, hurting others or yourself.

Emotions are okay, but they are not to control you. You are to control your emotions. Emotions are there to be our barometer to measure the pressure within us. They help us navigate our situations.

It is how we use that essential tool; will I learn from this or allow it to overtake me?

Proverbs 12:15 says the way of the fool is right in his own eyes. God gave us our feelings and emotions for a reason. Living by faith doesn't mean we ignore them. They are not evil by themselves, but what we allow our thoughts to dwell on.

Dwell is key here, are you going to stay in this place? How long are you going to allow yourself to stay in the hurt and pain? Do you have a choice? Yes! You are in control of your thoughts and emotions and when you aren't...well you lost control and you need saving, help and it's not drugs or addictive substances.

By changing your negative into; okay here's the situation and what is my resolution going to be? You can set a new course, have a plan and begin seeing past those clouds. You cannot allow them to overtake you.

Call your thoughts into submission, hold them captive and go to the word of God and ask okay Lord, your word says; "When the enemy comes in like a flood, The Spirit of the Lord will lift up a standard against him. - Isaiah 59:19.

Do you think speaking Assertively is aggression? One speaks with confidence the other attacks.

Assertive: having or showing a confident and forceful personality.

Aggressive: ready or likely to attack or confront; characterized by or resulting from aggression.

When we speak with assertiveness, we demonstrate our confidence in what we are saying. With respect, care and empathy.

When we speak with Aggression, we are speaking at someone with anger or malice.

We have learned to listen to understand, but now we must speak understanding with respect, care and empathy.

C answer with confidence
A answer with love
R answer with respect
E answer with empathy

Proverbs 15:4 "Gentle words bring life and health; a deceitful tongue crushes the spirit."

Proverbs 16:24 "Kind words are like honey—sweet to the soul and healthy for the body." ...

Proverbs 18:20 "Words satisfy the soul as food satisfies the stomach; the right words on a person's lips bring satisfaction."

Your words can crush or bring life to your lips and when you speak life... everyone wins.

1 Corinthians 3:18 Let no one deceive himself. If any of you thinks he is wise in the ways of this world, he must become a fool to become really wise.

God's ways are not the worlds ways. His ways are not our ways.

1John 2:15 Do not love the world or anything in the world. If anyone loves the world, love for the Father is not in them.

Romans 12:2 Do not conform to the pattern of this world, but be transformed by the renewing of your mind. Then you will be able to test and approve what God's will is—his good, pleasing and perfect will.

What good is it for someone to gain the whole world, yet forfeit their soul? Mark 8:36

I have told you these things, so that in me you may have peace. In this world you will have trouble. But take heart! I have overcome the world. John 6:33

For the grace of God has appeared that offers salvation to all people. It teaches us to say "No" to ungodliness and worldly passions, and to live self-controlled, upright and godly lives in this present age. Titus 2:11-12

For though we live in the world, we do not wage war as the world does. 2 Corinthians 10:3

What do all of these scriptures say? God's ways are not carnal, His ways are not man's ways. He tells us to obey the laws, but who do we obey 1st? God! If it doesn't line up with His word...I don't want it.

Be careful what you hear, be careful what you see for our eyes, ears and minds can be deceived, but if you line it up with the Bible and it conforms to His word...well then, it's alright with me.

God 1st, His ways, His Will and His word is what I follow.

What are you listening to? Who are you listening to? Who is controlling your mind?

As for me and my house, I shall serve the Lord.

Trust, without it you can't build a relationship, with it you have this unwavering...I know, that I know; they have my back. You believe in the reliability, truth, ability, or the strength of that person.

Trust has to be built upon through relationships. The more you get to know that person, you either build more trust or they show you they are untrustworthy.

When that trust is broken, it can be devastating, like a shattering... can you ever trust again?

We are human and there will be times of believing in someone's ability of being trustworthy and others where we question it.

But there is One that will always shine above the rest. He will never forsake you, but it will cost you everything. The relationship you build with Him will be worth it.

When His Love came down, He knew what His mission here on earth was for; you and me. To extinguish our sin on the Cross, so that we can trust Him, believe in Him, in His ability and power.

What Jesus did wasn't easy and He knew it, but yet He said Father your will be done.

Trusting in someone isn't easy, but it is the cornerstone in a relationship. Without trust you cannot build a relationship.

Let Jesus show you His reliability, His truth, His ability, and His strength. You will be forever changed.

Forgiveness defined by Webster's is; to cease to feel resentment against (an offender) to pardon, to forgive one's enemies, to give up resentment.

The Bible's definition is including but not limited to remit (a debt), to leave (something or someone) alone, to allow (an action), to leave, to send away...to send away unforgiveness.

So many feelings are tied to unforgiveness. Hurt, pain, tears shed...all so draining. Could you imagine what your life would look like today if you learned and mastered forgiveness?

To leave it, to allow it to go or to send unforgiveness away.

The words are easy to read but the act of forgiveness is difficult to do, why?

Because our emotions are still tied to the event. Our memory is stuck on repeat in our hearts and mind. Especially for women, we live in the moment and our emotions are always felt deeply, therefore our emotions are bound to the past. It's harder for a woman to forgive, but not impossible to learn how to let go.

Webster's say to cease (stop) to feel resentment against. When your tears cease, the hurt stops and you let go, you have forgiven.

The above doesn't say you forget, but it takes an action from you, that you are willing to let go of that emotion or memory that has kept you chained and bound for all these years.

I choose to forgive, I choose to let go, I choose to release the offense and the offender(s), I choose to give up resenting, I choose to no longer be the victim, I choose to abandon the hurt and pain that has imprisoned me for so many years. I choose to break those generational curses upon me and my children and their children.

I choose love, kindness and forgiveness. I choose to live the rest of my days letting go of the past and living life today, in this moment, filled with self-compassion and love.

Empowering words...I choose!

Change is hard, working out is difficult and takes commitment to change your physic. You know what is harder, to begin healing your insides. This too takes courage to journey through your past, visit those sore and hurtful places and begin to heal the child within, or the teenager; whenever those crushing memories began.

We try so hard to forget by stuffing the days, weeks and even years, to the pits of our stomachs. No wonder so many of us have stomach issues.

Into the past you must go, like exhuming your dead parts, to be examined by the Great Physician so that He can light the path in your journey of healing. Only He can make dry bones...listen.

Psalm 34:18 The LORD is near to the brokenhearted and saves the crushed in spirit.

To begin admit you are powerless in yourself and need help.

Jeremiah 17:14 Heal me, Lord, and I will be healed; save me and I will be saved, for you are the one I praise.

Believe that He is close to you, He hears you and is there to forgive all.

Matthew 7:7-8 Ask and it will be given to you; seek and you will find; knock and the door will be opened to you.

And finally, ask Him into your heart, seek His heart, pray that He opens the door and begins a renewing of your mind. Ask the Holy Spirit to go through the cobwebs of your heart and begins to cleanup.

God is not only able to physically heal us, He is also able to cleanse us from all unrighteousness. All He requires of us is prayer.

Father, Jesus my Savior, my Comforter; I pray that you will comfort me in my suffering. Give me such confidence in the power of your grace, that even when I am afraid, I may put my whole trust in you. Am

Creeks, streams, rivers and oceans...water always flowing, moving from the smallest creeks to streams to rivers and onto the oceans. Waves crashing to shore and back out but always moving.

When a river dries out either too much construction was created at the mouth of the river and caused it to dry out. Creeks and streams can dry out too.

Just the right amount of rain replenishes our water sources. Too much causes flooding, mudslides and then stagnant water causes mold.

God created us to always be flowing, moving forward, being cleansed, renewed, and refreshed daily.

Too much busyness (Construction at the mouth of the river) causes our spirit to dry out.

Too much rest, being stuck in the past hurts and pains causes us to stagnate.

Today be renewed, everything in balance, keep growing, moving forward shod your feet in His word. Put on the full armor of God and learn how-to live-in Peace!

Be like a river flowing into the vast ocean of opportunities.

Trust when it's broken, you feel as if everything you heard, saw and know up this this moment is a lie. Trust is unseen but a tie that binds 2 people together with this mutual ideal...I trust you.

Some people trust right off the bat; some people make you work for their trust and others show you straight away they are/or not trustworthy.

If they show you that you can rely on them, you begin to build your trust in them. If they show you the opposite, you question every move they make.

Trust has to be the cornerstone of any relationship without it, the relationship is built on sand.

Ever watch court TV? As soon as the judge catches either the plaintiff or the defendant in a lie, the judge cannot believe anything that person said. 1 lie can tear at the very foundation of a relationship. It is the hardest thing to repair.

Can it be repaired? Yes, but it takes work, love and a lot of mercy and grace on both sides. But if we can be forgiven by our Father in heaven, then we can be kind and gracious to our fellow man and forgive.

Remember forgiveness doesn't mean you forget, but you release that tie that has kept you bound.

Trust in the Lord with all your heart!